Dog-friendly gardening

Hubble & Hattie

Karen Bush

Creating a safe haven for you and your dog

www.hubbleandhattie.com

The Hubble & Hattie imprint was launched in 2009 and is named in memory of two very special Westies owned by Veloce's proprietors.

Since the first book, many more have been added to the list, all with the same underlying objective: to be of real benefit to the species they cover, at the same time promoting compassion, understanding and co-operation between all animals (including human ones!)

Hubble & Hattie is the home of a range of books that cover all-things animal, produced to the same high quality of content and presentation as our motoring books, and offering the same great value for money.

3 1561 00283 9417

DEDICATION

This is for two special people – in memory of my Dad, who started it all off with a packet of pansy seeds, and for Sarah Fisher who has made a huge difference to the lives of countless dogs and other animals, and whose dedication and enthusiasm is an inspiration to all those who meet her.

Chapter start photo courtesy *Your Dog*/Bob Atkins

First published in July 2012 by Veloce Publishing Limited, Veloce House, Parkway Farm Business Park, Middle Farm Way, Poundbury, Dorchester, Dorset, DT1 3AR, England. Fax 01305 250479/e-mail info@hubbleandhattie.com/web www.hubbleandhattie.com
ISBN: 978-1-845844-10-3 UPC: 6-36847-04410-7 © Karen Bush & Veloce Publishing Ltd 2012. All rights reserved. With the exception of quoting brief passages for the purpose of review, no part of this publication may be recorded, reproduced or transmitted by any means, including photocopying, without the written permission of Veloce Publishing Ltd. Throughout this book logos, model names and designations, etc, have been used for the purposes of identification, illustration and decoration. Such names are the property of the trademark holder as this is not an official publication.
Readers with ideas for books about animals, or animal-related topics, are invited to write to the editorial director of Veloce Publishing at the above address. British Library Cataloguing in Publication Data – A catalogue record for this book is available from the British Library. Typesetting, design and page make-up all by Veloce Publishing Ltd on Apple Mac. Printed in India by Replika Press Ltd

Contents

Acknowledgements • Foreword • Introduction

Acknowledgements

A lot of people helped with this book, and a big thank you is due to the many friends as well as to all the Tellington-Touch instructors, practitioners and trainees who so generously shared ideas, stories and pictures, including:

Kathy Allison, Bob Atkins, Hilda Bootsmann, Val Borland, Maxine Bray, Jacqui Carter, Victoria Colville, Claire Colvin, Tina Constance, Mags Denness, Julii Elliott, Claudette Evans, Janet Finlay, Sarah Fisher, Keith Gullis, Ali Hetherington, Bill Hinton, Garry Hinton, Rachel Jackson, Anita Janssen, Kerry Jenkinson, Deborah Kieboom, Ali Knight, Jon Langley, Sally Long, Rachael Manns, Sarah Marsh, Will Marsh, Angie McCue, Marie Miller, Emma Mitchell, Shona Moon, Corinne Moore, Megan Moore, Ben Page, Lisa Page, Claire Pearson, Briony Price, Hayley Price, Julie Sadler, Toni Shelbourne, Kevin Spurgeon, Straid Veterinary Clinic, Anne Whitfield, Sarah Wright. And Andy Jones for last-miniute kennel pic!

Special thanks also go to Julie Webb – thanks for all your patience! – and to my two office assistants and head gardeners, Archie and Angel.

✿ ✿ ✿ ✿ ✿

Foreword by Anthony Head

I love dogs – I really love them. Big ones, little ones, long ones, round ones. I love their intrepid characters, their extraordinary expressiveness. When I see a dog walking along the street, I'm always captivated by their unfaltering loyalty to their owner – a genuine pleasure at being by his or her side. You can see it in their faces; as they go through a myriad of expressions reacting to all the various stimuli that they encounter, one overriding emotion prevails – one of pride or love or something quite overwhelming that seems to stem from the bond they feel with us, the human race.

Many of the problems that owners encounter with their dogs derive from boredom, stress or anxiety. If we give them outlets for their natural drives and desires and encourage them to play, 'work' and problem-solve, we can further enhance their lives – and ours.

It follows, therefore, that we should do our utmost to enrich their environment and to continue to build bonds between us that will last a lifetime, not just in the home but in the garden, too. The garden does not have to be just a place to stretch their legs, or take that last wee before bedtime. It can be somewhere that our canine friends can enjoy as much as we do, and this brilliant book will give you some new ideas, expand on old ones, and above all help to keep your beloved dog safe.

Karen Bush is a dear friend and, like me and my partner, Sarah, a consummate dog lover. I am truly honoured that she asked me to write this foreword. Without a doubt this book should be on the bookshelf of every dog owner. Your dog will thank you for it.

Anthony Head.
(Courtesy Sarah Fisher)

Introduction

Walk into any bookshop or library and, whilst you'll find vast numbers of gardening books stacked on the shelves, most of them won't offer much by way of helpful advice for dog owners. When pets are mentioned, it's often in the context of them being pests rather than much-loved companions.

This book aims to help you find a way of successfully combining both dog and garden, and as well as looking at solutions to age-old problems such as dealing with urine burns on the lawn, also offers suggestions for how you can make your plot more dog-friendly: a stimulating, fun, and above all, safe place for him to be. All of the advice relating to medical treatment has been checked and approved by a veterinary surgeon.

Even if you don't really consider yourself a gardener, as you begin taking a more active interest in your garden – purely for your dog's benefit, of course – you may find it triggers a hitherto unsuspected gardening gene. If not, don't worry: your efforts will still be appreciated by your canine friend!

Making a start

Like interior decorating, garden design goes through fashions; it's also a highly personal thing and your tastes may be very different from those of others. Go with whatever makes you (and your dog) happy, and pleases your own eye rather than feel you have to follow the latest trends.

If your idea of perfection is a fence-to-fence lawn, that's fine – it also makes design very simple! But adding a few features can transform a rather boring and bare space into a much more interesting and fun place for your dog. If you want to stick with a minimalist lawn, these 'features' can be portable objects which can be moved around or stored when not in use (see the chapter *Enjoying the garden*). If more permanent elements such as water, patios, steps, and flower beds and borders are what you have in mind, then spend a little time planning them out, as this will help you to avoid making major mistakes and wasting time, money and effort.

DESIGN

If you're starting with a clean slate and like technology, you may find one of the garden design software programmes handy. You can pick up a bargain on Amazon, and also read reviews as to how helpful and easy to use each product is.

Visiting gardens that are open to the public can make a nice day out, as well as provide inspiration for ideas you can incorporate into your own garden – although possibly on a less grandiose scale. Some, such as Coombe Trenchard in Devon, admit dogs, so you may be able to take your canine friend along as well: check before you set out. This is a family pet – you will usually be expected to keep your own on a leash. (Courtesy Will Marsh)

Alternatively, a sheet of graph paper can be used to work out your design. Take into account all your dog's requirements first, and then add in your own; you'll find suggestions for features and planting in the following chapters that you may like to incorporate into your plan. If you're not quite sure how to set about getting your ideas down on paper there are lots of books available which will guide you through the technical parts of the process. Don't be tempted to skip this step if you have a small garden, as the less space you have, the more important it is to plan carefully in order to use what is available both wisely and well.

Unless your garden is in a pretty bad state, it's unlikely that you will be starting from scratch: for most of us it's a case of working with what we have and within a budget; spreading the acquisition and cost of design features over a period of time. Watching your garden gradually evolve can be one

of the great pleasures of gardening, however, and, once you're hooked, no-one will ever be short of ideas for presents for you on birthdays or at Christmas!

How much effort you want to put into keeping your garden looking good is entirely up to you, but it's definitely something to bear in mind when designing your ideal space. It's perfectly possible to have a stunning show garden if you enjoy gardening and have the time to devote to it, but if you're a busy person (or a lazy gardener), look at ways of incorporating interesting features which are low-maintenance – be very honest with yourself about how much time you have available and the amount of effort you'll be happy to put in on a consistent basis. A sculptural, grassy mound or seat, for example, can look spectacular and be a fun feature for your dog – but only if you're prepared to regularly wield the shears to cut it by hand. Allow it to become overgrown and not only will it quickly become unsightly, it could also be a potential hazard to your dog if he misjudges a jump onto or off it.

When creating a garden that is going to satisfy all (or at any rate, most) of your dog's requirements, it helps if you have a reasonably clear idea what sort of things he'd put at the top of his wish list. Quite likely it would include good places to dig, somewhere to snooze, interesting things to sniff at, places to scent mark, smelly stuff to roll in, rubbish to scavenge through ... Obviously, some of these activities aren't going to be acceptable to you, but once you're aware of the sort of things he'd like to do, you can think up methods of channelling these perfectly natural doggy urges in ways which will help keep him content while ensuring your garden doesn't become a rank and unpleasant eyesore.

WHAT DOGS WANT

As most literature about choosing a dog will tell you, some types and breeds are associated with particular inherited behaviours: for example, terriers are renowned for their digging prowess, sighthounds for zooming around at high speed,

Puppies are curious about everything – and don't necessarily grow out of it as they get older. (Courtesy www. photographybybenpage. co.uk)

Newfoundlands for their affinity with water, and Labradors for their seemingly tireless desire to chase balls.

Although this means that you can to a certain extent predict some behaviours based on knowledge of what job your dog was traditionally bred to do, remember that these characteristics are only guidelines, not hard-and-fast predictions, and aren't even necessarily breed-exclusive traits, either. One of my own whippets will dig with as much determination and enthusiasm as a terrier, while the other is as ball-oriented as any Labrador. Regardless of breed, therefore, it's more important to observe your dog as an individual rather than a generalisation, as this will help you decide what sort of garden features and activities will best cater for his particular passions in life.

Canine characteristics
Having said that, there are however, certain attributes which are common to all canines, and will have a bearing on dog-friendly garden design and management:

✿ Insatiable curiosity
Most dogs are inquisitive and will investigate anything new in the garden with great interest.

Dogs will make their own entertainment if you don't provide it for them. (Courtesy Sally Long)

This curiosity about their surroundings is especially evident in puppies, who will find out more by using their mouths as well as their other senses. Just because your dog has outgrown the puppy chewing phase doesn't mean he won't continue to use his mouth and teeth on occasion to check out something. For this reason you'll need to cultivate the habit of being a tidy gardener, ensuring that anything potentially dangerous is kept safely out of his reach. Your garden will, of course, change with the seasons, which alone will make it an interestingly varied environment, but your dog will also enjoy finding occasional 'surprises' you've placed out there for him to discover – just make sure they're intentional ones

✿ Vision, scent and hearing

Compared with humans, dogs are short-sighted and red/green colour blind, although their sight *is* very sensitive to movement, as well as much better than ours in poor light. The canine sense of smell is considerably more powerful than ours, with around 200 million scent detecting receptors in his nose compared to our paltry five million; hearing is also far greater in range. This means that while a colourful display of flowers is visually stimulating to us, it's of less importance to your dog – plants which smell, or foliage which moves gently in the breeze will be far more interesting. Your dog's sensitivity to sound and movement can also become a problem in some cases if he becomes over-stimulated, or even territorial about anything

he can see or hear on the other side of the garden fence: people walking by, for example. This means that as well as erecting dog-proof fencing, you'll also need to give consideration to screening off the outside world, training, and the times he's allowed in the garden.

✿ Intelligence

Dogs are anything but dumb friends, and lack of mental stimulation is as likely to lead to a trashed garden as insufficient exercise. A bored dog will invent his own entertainment, whether it's digging under or climbing over the fence, destroying your garden furniture or barking non-stop. They're also essentially social animals, and can become lonely if constantly left to mooch around outside on their own. While providing lots of interesting features will help occupy him and make the garden a more fun place to be, don't view them as a substitute for proper walks or for spending quality time interacting with each other.

Plus ...

To this basic overview you also need to consider and add any requirements specific to your dog: a very small one may have trouble with high steps, for example, while careful siting of pots, statuary and greenhouses will be needed with a dog who likes to race around madly, and erecting an external mailbox might be wise with a dog with guardian tendencies.

Some dogs may be 'special needs' with sight, hearing or mobility issues, so careful thought must be given to how you can make the garden a safe environment for him. As your dog becomes more elderly, these afflictions are increasingly likely, and you may need to make changes or adapt certain elements of your garden (see also the chapter on *Garden features*).

WHAT DO YOU WANT?

As you would also like to enjoy your garden, it doesn't hurt to scribble your own 'wish list' – maybe you've always fancied a water feature, would like a barbecue area for al fresco dining, attractive

The garden should be a place for both of you to share and enjoy together. (Courtesy Corinne Moore/Tina Constance)

flowers and possibly even a few home-grown veggies – and then consider ways that some or all of these can be safely incorporated.

Some compromise may be necessary (although the safety and wellbeing of you and your dog should be your priority), but with a little thought and imagination it's usually possible to arrive at a solution that everyone can live with. Don't forget, too, that although you are aiming to create a dog-friendly garden, you should also be prepared to put some effort into producing a garden-friendly dog, which can include teaching a 'wee' command, or training him to keep off the flower beds. Of course,

a dog who is both well-exercised and well-trained will be more content, and less likely to lay waste to all your handiwork.

OTHER GARDEN USERS
Don't forget to give some thought to other garden users, such as children; you may decide to split the space to create a separate child-only play area which your dog isn't allowed in. If you have other pets who use the garden, consider their needs and welfare also. Emma Mitchell's dog, Cloutie, is happy to simply watch the bunnies and guinea pigs in their enclosure, and they're quite relaxed about

Cloutie keeps an eye on the small furries that share the garden. (Courtesy Emma Mitchell)

being under her scrutiny. But not all dogs are so good-natured, and the presence of a potentially predatory animal close by can be highly stressful for many small furries. Secure fencing around them may not be enough, and you might need to exclude your dog altogether from the area where they're kept.

Keeping your dog safe

Fencing can be one of the most expensive investments you make in your garden, but for dog owners it's also one of the most essential, helping to keep pets contained and safe.

FENCING

Although budget may dictate the type of fencing you choose, it should still be sturdy and high enough – and with some dogs, deep enough, too – to do the job of keeping your pet within the garden.

Ideally, a solid fence is best, whether of stone, brick or wooden fence panels, since as well as giving you a degree of privacy, it helps prevent constant visual stimulation that some dogs may find hard to cope with. Even if dogs or people passing on the other side pay him no attention, they can still be difficult for him to ignore, and if he is constantly running up and down the fenceline guarding his territory, he is going to be in a continual state of stress and high arousal. This will not resolve by itself (see *Visitors*, page 17), and if anyone actually tries to be friendly and say hello, there's a risk that they may get nipped.

If you have fencing with gaps in it (such as railings or chain link), erecting some kind of screening will help make it a more peaceful haven

Some dogs love to watch the world go by – but for others, being able to see passersby through gaps in the fencing can be stressful. (Courtesy Will Marsh)

Some dogs can be incredibly agile and athletic, and may put these skills to use in escaping from the garden. (Courtesy Claire Colvin)

for your dog; I suggest that you don't leave your dog outdoors unattended – for his own safety and that of others – until you've been able to do so. Depending on your tastes and what you can afford, screens of mesh, woven willow or birch panels are options, and can also be used to increase height: alternatively, use planting in the form of shrubs.

A hedge can also create a wonderful screen, although it may take a while to establish, during which time it will need protection from your dog. Even if it is mature, dense and prickly, don't rely on it as the sole method of containment, as he will invariably discover any weak spots that appear long before you do, and if the temptation is strong enough, may push through to the other side, regardless of discomfort.

Where friction exists between your dog and that of a neighbour in an adjoining garden, be prepared to create a really solid barrier, such as a wall or sheet metal fence between the properties:

anything less may be destroyed in their efforts to reach each other.

Although screening off the outside world so it can't be seen will help, your dog will still be able to hear what's going on (and, depending on the height of the fence, still be able to see the heads of people walking past), so you may need to do some training with him as well. Teach a good recall cue so you can call him to you if necessary, and divert his attention elsewhere. Setting up a Tellington-Touch 'confidence course' can help him develop self-control and calmness in potentially stressful situations when others are passing by (see also *Enjoying the garden*), and you can also make sure there are plenty of rewarding things to engage his interest within the garden. If you find yourself struggling with this, seek help from a behavioural trainer rather than risk matters getting progressively worse.

Height

How high your fence should be depends on the size of your dog and his athletic ability (which can often be much greater than you think!). Whilst a height of 4ft (1.2m) might be fine for most canines, 6ft (1.8m) may be necessary for large breeds. In the UK, planning permission isn't normally needed to erect a fence or wall unless it exceeds 6ft 6in (2m), or 3ft 3in (1m) if situated next to a road, footpath or pavement, but check covenants, nevertheless, just in case there are any special restrictions.

New fencing

If you're thinking of erecting new fencing, check for any local regulations on type and height – or indeed, on putting up any form of barrier at all. Then check your property deeds to determine where the boundaries are: all supporting posts should be entirely on your property and not encroach on that of your neighbours'.

If a fence which divides your property from that of your neighbour belongs to him, even though it butts up against your boundary, legally you can only hang things on it, add trellis, or use it as a support for plants if he gives you permission to do so: this also applies to staining, painting or applying preservative on your side – a good reason for staying on friendly terms with him! You can, of course, plant free-standing shrubs and other plants next to it, or if necessary erect your own fence alongside on your property.

'Invisible' fences

'Invisible' – also known as 'containment' – fencing usually consists of a wire installed around the perimeter of the area where you want your dog to stay, and which activates a sensor in a special collar that he wears. As he approaches the boundary, the collar warns him by vibrating or making a noise, and if he continues or tries to cross, it administers an electric shock.

It is a deeply unpleasant and inhumane system to inflict on your dog or any animal, and happily, electric shock collars have now been banned in Austria, Denmark, Germany, Slovenia, Switzerland, parts of Australia and in Wales, and at the time of writing are under review in the rest of the UK which, hopefully, will soon follow suit.

As well as causing physical pain to your canine friend, this system does nothing to keep other people or animals out of your garden, leaving your dog vulnerable to teasing or attack at any time. Should he become sufficiently scared or aroused by something, he may run across the barrier anyway, and will then be stuck on the wrong side of it, reluctant to pass over it again. Quite apart from this aspect, the systems are not failproof, and can malfunction: incidents have been reported where severe burns have been caused, and if you forget to remove the collar when leaving your property with your dog on the leash or in the car, he will be accidentally shocked. If he runs to greet approaching people, he may also get zapped and therefore assume that the arrival of visitors is a bad thing, and act aggressively toward them.

Shock collars, quite rightly, have been denounced by many major welfare and training organisations, and scientific research reinforces their stance on the physical and psychologically harmful effects. If you care about your dog, please

Never fall into the trap of underestimating your dog's ability to squeeze through the tightest of spaces. (Courtesy Garry Hinton/Keith Gullis)

do not even consider installing one of these systems!

GATES

Gates can be a weak link in your perimeter fence – don't underestimate your dog's ability to wriggle through the tightest of spaces. Leave the smallest possible amount of clearance necessary to be able to open the gate, and if he's a climber, get one which either offers no purchase for paws, or has an angled top (see below, *Escape artists*). If he prefers to tunnel, place slabs or concrete beneath it.

Some dogs learn how to lift latches, and even slide bolts across, so either position them too high for him to reach, or fit a fully enclosed pony-proof bolt of the sort used on stable doors. When access isn't needed, use a padlock to prevent unauthorised entry.

Even though the gate may be escape-proof in normal circumstances, it can still be inadvertently left open or not closed properly, so a spring closer might be a good idea. A 'Please close the gate' reminder sign can help, too! If the gate opens on to a main road, or your dog is liable to dart out past you when you open it, fitting double entry gates should keep him safely on the right side of them.

Escape artists

There are many reasons why dogs might try to escape from gardens, including fear, boredom,

Now kept safely contained in her own garden, Mirri enjoys the sun as she waits for unsuspecting people to fall into her carefully crafted 'heffalump trap' that you can see in the foreground. Behind her can be seen her owner, Janet's, even more carefully constructed dog-proof fence! (Courtesy Janet Finlay)

extraordinary clips on YouTube which show dogs demonstrating some impressive climbing skills. Facing fencing that offers toeholds (such as chain link, trellis, or vertical fence panels) with a smooth surface that offers no purchase for paws may deter climbers, or, as Janet Finlay discovered (see below), probably the most effective solution for both climbers and jumpers is to fit angled brackets around the top of the fence. These can either be at right angles or angled upward at 45 degrees, with wire running between them to support mesh or netting. Don't forget the gate, which will also need the same makeover.

Not all dogs go over the top in search of freedom – some will tunnel underneath. There are several ways you can try foiling this; probably the easiest is to pave around the inside perimeter of the fence. Another is to dig a trench along the base of the fence which is around 6in (15cm) deep and 12in (30cm) wide: line it with small-holed wire mesh, stapling the top edge to the fence, and then refilling with soil. A really tenacious dog may injure himself trying to bite or dig through this, in which case, dig the trench again, but this time fill it with concrete which you can either make into an attractive feature by studding the surface with cobbles, shells or glass beads, or sink a little deeper than the surrounding ground and once set, cover with soil and turf. Remember to tunnelproof your gate, too!

Even though your dog may not have shown any interest so far in digging under the fence, any gaps between it and the ground may encourage him first of all to investigate more closely, and then to enlarge the gap, so block any before it gets to this point.

Garden solutions

Janet Finlay is no stranger to the worries of owning a Houdini-hound, as she explains: "I found our lurcher, Mirri, running loose during rush hour on the ring road in Leeds as a six-month-old pup. No-one claimed her so she stayed, although we soon learned how she came to be out on the road: she is a serious escape artist. Any sign or scent of

separation anxiety, loneliness, sex, or being teased by something on the other side of the fence.

Remedying the underlying cause and ensuring your dog has sufficient exercise can help, but even then, some just seem to have an overwhelming desire to be on the wrong side of the fence. Making the fence too high to jump may solve the problem for some: using shrubs or hedging along it may also work, but beware placing objects such as benches or pots nearby which may be used as stepping stones. Keep an especially careful eye on your dog in the winter if there are heavy snowfalls, as drifts against the fence can also make it conveniently lower.

Don't underestimate the ingenuity or ability of a determined dog either: there are quite a fox, and she would scale our fence; she would also chase after cats and squirrels who came into the garden. Although at five foot, our fencing wasn't low, neither was it high enough to keep her in. We tried increasing the height to two metres, and thought we'd cracked it, but then she'd find a spot where she could scale it and be out again. Each time we found her escape route we'd barricade it, only for her to find somewhere else! The last time she got out she was injured quite badly, but thankfully we found her in time and she made a full recovery. But it was the last straw – we *had* to find a way to keep her in.

"A friend suggested creating an overhang, and then kindly made it for us: a series of angled supports facing inward along the fence have heavy gauge wire and mesh strung between them, which is also securely stapled to the top of the fence so there are no gaps. Mirri has since tried to jump out – the first time was in pursuit of a squirrel. She leapt up the fence, bounced off the mesh and fell back down – she looked confused, tried again, and once more got bounced off. She picked herself up, shook herself and wandered off with a rather sheepish 'Squirrel? What squirrel?' look on her face ... She has tried a couple more times after provocation from the neighbourhood fox, but hasn't managed to escape yet, so – touch wood – we've finally found a solution that works."

FIREWORKS AND THUNDERSTORMS

Getting caught outdoors while fireworks are being let off can frighten your dog so badly that, in blind panic, he may succeed in escaping what is normally a perfectly secure garden. Keep him safely indoors at night during those times of year when you know fireworks are likely to be let off: whilst you can't prevent your neighbours from holding their own displays, you can at least try to stay on good terms with them, and ask that they warn you of any planned displays so that you can be prepared.

Thunderstorms can be just as terrifying for many dogs, so keep an eye on weather forecasts, and keep your dog indoors if storms are predicted.

One other aerial hazard that can be alarming for some dogs are hot air balloons. If you live in an area where they frequently pass overhead, think carefully about whether it is safe for your dog to be outdoors unsupervised.

CREATIVE CAMOUFLAGE

There's no reason why fencing can't be both effective *and* attractive. Planting climbers is an obvious way of brightening up your perimeters, although take care that plants or supports don't offer handy toeholds for climbing dogs (see *Escape artists*). As well as flowers, the garden fence can be a great place to grow fruit – loganberries, blackberries and raspberries can all be trained up against it, or maybe try a kiwi fruit: these can be very rampant and will grow fast, and have a certain dramatic Jack-and-the-Beanstalk quality. Fan-trained fruit trees can look wonderful: as well as decorative blossom in spring there will be fruit later in the year, and even when the leaves have fallen, the architectural framework of the bare branches can look striking.

A hedge can also look good, providing a habitat for wildlife as well as helping to screen the outside world, muffle sound, and act as a windbreak. You don't need to stick to just one species, either: a variety of plants can be used to add colour and create interest throughout the year. If you already have an existing hedge you might consider planting a climbing or rambling rose which can be woven through it, and will reward you with colour and scent.

Most hedges need a little tidying up at some point during the year; as well as being neater, clipping them back can encourage stronger, denser growth. Choose a time of year when you won't disturb any nesting birds – before the end of February – and if it needs attention again later on in the year, wait until September. It is illegal to damage or destroy a nest while it is being built or occupied. Collect up and dispose carefully of clippings, as your dog may be more likely to pick them up or chew on them if left lying around.

Not all of the fenceline needs to be taken up with planting: maybe you might like to add garden

15

Hedge clippings can prove more interesting to your dog than the hedge. (Courtesy Sally Long)

art (see *Garden features*), and – provided you don't have an escape artist – it can be a great place to put a seat or bench, so you have somewhere to sit and enjoy your garden. If you don't want to sacrifice planting space along the fenceline, simply position your seat in the centre of an archway to create an eye-catching arbour.

PLANTING SUGGESTIONS
✿ Nasturtiums (*Tropaeolum spp*)
One of the easiest and most versatile of climbers to grow. Either train up a fence or grow in baskets hung on the fence with brackets to allow the spectacular streamers of colour to flow over the edge and spill downward. The leaves are

an attractive fresh green colour, or you can buy varieties with variegated leaves if you prefer

✿ Star Jasmine (*Trachelospermum jasminoides*)
Can be a lovely climber for sheltered spots in mild regions; the dark evergreen foliage makes the perfect foil for the profusion of white, star-like flowers produced in mid to late summer which smell as good as they look

✿ Mahonia (*Mahonia aquifolium*)
Also known as Oregon Grape, this plant has an exotic look, but is easy to grow, and tolerant of almost any soil. The clusters of yellow flowers brighten up the dullest of days in early spring, and

can be a source of nectar and pollen for black caps and blue tits. The purple-blue clusters of berries can be used to make jam: better still, leave them for blackbirds and mistle thrushes to breakfast on

✿ Forsythia (*Forsythia spp*)
Another shrub which can be used as a hedging plant, and produces a glorious show of brilliant yellow flowers in early spring

Plants to avoid using as hedges or screening include Cherry laurel (*Prunus laurocerasus*), Yew (*Taxus spp*), Rhododendron (*Rhododendron spp*), and Oleander (*Nerium oleander*), which can all be fatal if eaten; death from Privet (*Ligustrum vulgare*) is rare but not unknown, while Box (*Buxus spp*) can make your dog feel pretty ill if he nibbles at it.

VISITORS

Even though your dog usually has a friendly disposition, he may act differently if an uninvited stranger sets foot on what he regards as his territory, especially if you aren't around. He may bark as the person approaches, and, when they leave, assume that it's because his strategy worked. The more often this happens, the more established the behaviour becomes, and it can soon escalate into nipping or biting to encourage the 'intruder' to depart more quickly. Although it might be possible to minimise this behaviour, it can be difficult – and probably unlikely – that you'll be able to completely eliminate it, so you'll need to have a way of keeping visitors safe.

A mailbox erected outside your garden will ensure *your* postman doesn't become one of the 5000 who are attacked each year in the UK while on their rounds, and will also preclude any possibility of gates being left open and allowing your dog to escape. To cope with tradesmen making grocery, milk or parcel deliveries, or other visitors, rig up an alarm system and put a notice on the gate asking them not to enter but to ring and wait for you to respond. Call your dog in so your visitor is safe; bear in mind that there are many anti-dog laws nowadays, and it isn't even necessary

Forsythia can add spring colour to hedges, or be used to help screen fences.

There's no reason why a mailbox can't be fun as well as functional. (Courtesy Sarah Fisher)

17

A collar with ID information can facilitate the speedy return of your dog if he escapes or becomes lost.

need to weigh up the chances of possible injury to your dog.

Security

The best way to safeguard your dog while he's in the garden is to keep an eye on him at all times when he's out there. Don't rely on him being able to look after himself; if an intruder really wants to enter your property he will, and your dog may be injured as a result. Make sure access gates are properly secured, keep fencing in good repair, ensure your dog has some kind of permanent ID (see below), and invest in security measures such as an alarm system and a motion sensor-operated light in the garden.

If, despite your best efforts, the worst happens and your dog escapes or is stolen:

❀ Notify the police and your local dog warden – supply them with recent photographs
❀ Contact veterinary practices in the area and ask staff to keep an eye out; if you can, put up a poster on their noticeboard
❀ Contact all animal rescue organisations in the area
❀ Approach local media including newspapers, TV and radio
❀ Ring your insurer as you may be able to claim assistance in offering a reward
❀ Put up posters with contact details and a good recent photograph
❀ Go online – there are many helpful websites which can offer advice and practical assistance in finding your pet
❀ Enlist the help of family and friends to search, allocating everyone a particular area

ID your dog

By law your dog must wear a collar displaying ID while out and about in public, and although not compulsory while in your own garden, it's prudent for him to do so, just in case he does escape. As a collar tag is also usually the first thing someone will look at if they find him, it can ensure that you are contacted more quickly. To minimise the risk of his

for your dog to actually bite someone for you to be prosecuted and him to be seized.

KEEP OUT!

As well as preventing your dog from straying, a garden fence helps to keep him from becoming a target for thieves. It's a sad fact that pet theft is on the increase, with dogs being stolen to order and either sold on, used in puppy farms or vivisection laboratories, or held to ransom.

Additional security features such as anti-climb spikes can also be helpful in deterring cats and squirrels, and prevent them from using fence tops as a walkway between gardens. As you may be liable if a member of the public suffers damage or injury from such fixtures, a warning sign should be placed where it is clearly visible. A prickly hedge can also be an effective deterrent, although you will collar getting caught up on something and injuring or strangling him, use a non-tightening flat collar which incorporates a safety breakaway section.

Because collars can sometimes become separated from your dog – or intentionally removed if he is stolen – a further means of permanent identification is also a sensible precaution. This can be done by tattooing the skin in an ear or on the belly or inner thigh (ears are not always the best place as it is not unknown for them to be cut off to prevent identification), or microchipping. A microchip is a tiny device, about the size of a grain of rice, which is implanted beneath the skin, and has a unique code number that can be read by a special, hand-held scanner and used to identify you as the owner. Although there have been occasional hiccups with this system, these have been minimal, and on the whole it has proved an effective and easy way to reunite lost pets with owners (and is compulsory for foreign travel with your dog).

MAINTENANCE

The best fence in the world will become useless if it's poorly maintained. Check regularly for weak areas – a small gap can rapidly become large enough to escape through if your dog discovers it first and decides to enlarge it. Replace and repair rotted posts or wobbly panels before the wind blows them down or your dog pushes them over; if you can't attend to it immediately, keep a close eye on your pet while he's outdoors, or if necessary, keep him on a leash until the area is secure again.

Before using any preservatives, stains or paints on timber fencing, check that they are pet-friendly, as there is always a risk that surfaces they are applied to will be licked or chewed, and certain precautions may need to be taken during application, or while drying. If you need more information about safety and usage than is provided on the labelling, contact the manufacturer: see also the chapter *Garden surfaces*.

Mind the gap! Regularly check fencing for weak areas.

Living areas

If you have the space, an outdoor run can be useful: if there are toxic plants or other potential hazards in your garden, this allows your dog to have access to a part of it which can be made absolutely safe for him at those times when you can't keep a close eye on what he's up to. It can also provide an extra room for him to relax or play in, and if he can access it directly from the house, means he can let himself out when he needs to relieve himself.

He shouldn't be left in it for long periods of time, however, and it shouldn't be used as his fulltime accommodation: if you aren't prepared to share your life and your home with your dog, then don't get one in the first place.

Building a run

As with garden perimeter fencing, a run needs to be secure and capable of keeping your dog safely within it. Depending on the level of your DIY skills, you can design and build your own, buy a self-assembly kit, or pay someone to do the job for you.

If buying one, you'll find there's a huge choice, so do plenty of research and think through what will best suit you and your dog before spending your money. You should also check whether planning permission is needed, as this can sometimes be a bit of a grey area, and what you can and can't do may vary from one district to the next. Your local planning office should be able to advise you; don't forget that some housing developments may have legal covenants and restrictions, too.

Care needs to be taken over siting a run. If it is immediately next to a pedestrian thoroughfare,

Most dogs enjoy a den of their own. (Courtesy Andy Jones)

for example, the constant disturbance can make it a very stressful environment for your dog, which can adversely affect his wellbeing and behaviour in general, as well as leading to him barking excessively and disturbing neighbours (see page 22).

Furnishing a run

Give a little thought to how the run should be equipped to ensure that it's a space your dog will enjoy spending time in. As it is a relatively small area, the surface you choose will need to be durable enough to withstand a fair amount of wear and tear; grass will quickly become sparse and liable to turn into a marshy bog in wet weather. Bark chips, pea gravel and sand can be alternatives and are discussed in the chapter *Garden surfaces*, and you can always use more than one surface to create different areas within the run if you wish.

Unless your dog has been trained to use a specific area within the run for his toilet, it may be difficult to keep hygienic and odour-free, however, and mould can sometimes be a problem with organic materials. If you opt for concrete, use a rake to create a grippy surface when laying it; as concrete is porous and can harbour worm eggs as well as odours, it's a good idea to treat it with a sealant, too. Another option is rubber flooring, which can be obtained either as mats or rolls in a variety of thicknesses. A favourite these days with horse owners for use in stables, it is a more forgiving and less abrasive surface than concrete or stone slabs, is hardwearing, and can easily be washed down and disinfected. Choose a textured rather than smooth surface to provide better grip for both feet and paws when wet.

Although a kennel isn't essential, many dogs enjoy having a 'den' they can retreat to when they want peace and quiet. Choose from a traditional wooden kennel, or a more modern, low maintenance design made from fibreglass or plastic. Site it where wind and rain won't blow straight in, and raise it off the ground slightly so it doesn't flood. A mattress-type bed inside will make it cosy; use a cover made of waterproof fabric.

Add features such as a pool and activity toys to keep your Dog Zone interesting. (Courtesy Sarah Fisher)

Provide an outdoor bed or hammock, too, so your dog has a choice of place to snooze; a comfy bed is particularly important if the run flooring is hard, especially as your dog becomes older.

Provide a shaded area which will offer protection during wet weather if he goes out to relieve himself (see *Garden surfaces*), as well as from the sun on warm days. Remember that not all dogs are sensible enough to seek out shade in hot weather, so keep an eye on temperatures and send him indoors if necessary (see also *Garden emergencies*). Although an established tree or large shrub can do the job nicely, as the sun moves across the sky it may be effective for only part of the day, so some form of canopy will be more useful.

You can create a more stimulating environment by adding features such as a tunnel, digging pit

Dogs bark for all sorts of reasons – including pigeons landing on the roof of the garden shed – but your neighbours may not appreciate the noise if it is persistent.

or paddling pool, hiding a few treats for him to discover, and providing a few safe chewy and activity toys (see *Enjoying the garden*). Fresh water should always be available, and if you feed your dog in the run, remove his bowls and wash them when he's finished so that they don't attract flies or vermin – also collect and wash any toys that contained food once he's finished with them. You could add plants for him to graze on if he wishes (see *Plants for the garden*); plant them in large, wide-bottomed pots that can't be knocked over to prevent them being trampled or urinated on.

NUISANCE BARKING

Dogs bark for all sorts of reasons: frustration, excitement, boredom, loneliness, to attract attention, when afraid or if startled; also because of separation anxiety, and in older dogs sometimes due to senility (Canine Cognitive Dysfuntion).

If your dog is persistently noisy it is – understandably – likely to annoy neighbours, which, if they complain to your local authority, could result in prosecution.

You should be equally concerned about the reason why your dog is barking in the first place, as it indicates that he's unhappy about something. Ensuring he is well exercised and has a few activity toys to occupy him may be helpful, but bear in mind that dogs are social creatures, and if you leave him alone in the garden or his run for hours on end, he may well become noisy in protest at his isolation.

Dogs who suffer from separation anxiety can become deeply distressed when left on their own; if you think this is the cause of his excessive barking, enlist the help of a behavioural trainer who can advise on how to increase his ability to cope without you. Where senility is thought to be a contributary factor, consult your vet as there are several drugs which may help.

Your dog may also bark in response to stimuli caused by passersby he can hear or see through fencing; as previously mentioned, siting runs away from garden perimeters and using screening may solve the problem in some cases, but if not, you will need to restrict outdoor access to times when you are around and can take control of the situation. Do not assume that if you ignore him he will eventually get fed up with barking and stop: he won't. Very often, it becomes self-perpetuating, and the more he barks, the more he feels the need to continue.

HOUSE TO GARDEN ACCESS

If you want to allow your dog free access to the garden or a run, you need to be absolutely sure that it is a 100 per cent safe environment for him to be in, and totally escape-proof. Bearing in mind that this option can leave your dog vulnerable to thieves, and your house to burglars, you may decide that, for security reasons, it's best reserved for when someone is at home.

If fireworks or thundery weather are expected, restrict outdoor access, too, as the noise of these can be frightening for many dogs, and may cause them to panic.

Dog doors

A dog door is simply a larger version of a cat flap. Some are manually operated by your dog using his head to push a flap open, whilst others have sensors or magnets that respond to a signal from a special collar that your dog wears, opening when he is near, and automatically closing once he's gone through.

Depending on design, some flaps may not be very weatherproof, and manual flaps can admit other animals besides your dog. Doors obviously must be big enough to let your dog pass through comfortably, but if you have a large dog, this can mean that human intruders are able to get in as well. Although flaps can be locked, they are nevertheless a weak link, and may not be burglar-proof.

If leaving the door to your house open, ensure it is firmly wedged so that it can't close, accidentally trapping your dog outside. Obviously, if you are away from home, an open door can be even more of an invitation to thieves, so this course of action is not recommended.

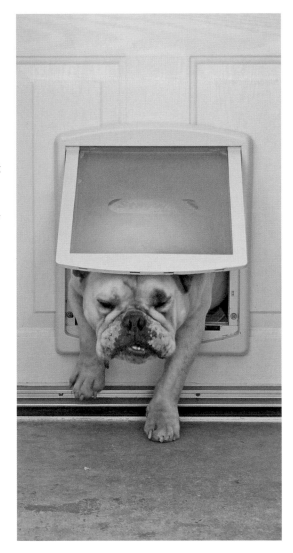

A dog flap will allow your dog free access to the garden.

GARDEN SOLUTION

If your dog isn't free to come and go as he pleases between house and garden, you can teach him to ring a bell to let you know when he wants to go out (or come back in again) – it will also save your door from claw marks. Try hanging a bell from a door handle, or, better still, buy a wireless doggy

23

Use decals or some form of marking on glazing to prevent your dog from running head first into glass windows and doors.

doorbell set: this consists of a pressure pad placed on the ground which sounds a plug-in internal doorchime when your dog touches it with a paw or his nose, so you'll hear it wherever you are in the house.

Door safety

It can be difficult for dogs to tell when glazed doors are open or shut, so prevent accidents happening by him running full tilt into it while closed by adding some kind of visible mark. If you have nothing else to hand, try strips of masking tape, but reusable decals such as the snowflake ones shown do the job and look decorative, too. This precaution will also help prevent birds from crashing into them – the RSPB sells a variety of reusable stickers.

CRATES AND PLAYPENS

A crate can be a handy way of safely containing a puppy or adult dog who can't be left safely to his own devices, at those times when you're busy and can't keep a close eye on him. He'll still be able to enjoy being outside with you, leaving you to concentrate on getting on with garden chores. If you have a puppy, you could use a doggy playpen if you prefer, which will give more room, although it needs to be sturdy and high enough that he can't climb or jump out.

Don't just put him in a crate and expect him to be happy about it: you'll need to create a pleasant environment and nice associations so that he is content to be there. Place some comfy bedding inside, and introduce the concept by feeding him in there. When he's likely to be tired and feeling ready for a snooze after a walk, encourage him to nap there by placing a few treats or maybe a stuffed Kong® for him to find. Don't shut the door until he is happy to relax and settle in there with it open.

Don't leave him confined for more than an hour; make sure he has shade and that fresh drinking water is available.

Leave him indoors instead on hot days or if conditions are humid as this makes it hard for him to lose heat efficiently (see also *Garden emergencies*).

Make your dog's crate
a place he enjoys.
(Courtesy Sarah Fisher)

TETHERING

Alternatively, you can use a corkscrew stake to tether your dog, which gives a little more freedom of movement than a crate, so may be preferable for dogs who are stiff and arthritic and need more room to manouevre. Do not try this with a young puppy, though, and as with a crate or play pen, make sure you provide shade in sunny weather, fresh water within easy reach, a comfy bed or a blanket to lie on, and a chewy treat, stuffed Kong® or similar toy to keep him occupied.

In the US, around twenty states place specific restrictions on how, when and where you are allowed to tether a dog, so check local legislation first.

Safety

Tether your dog for short periods only and while you are present – never leave him on his own in case he becomes entangled in the leash. It will also leave him vulnerable to teasing, theft, stress, or even attack if other people or animals come into the garden during your absence. If you need to go indoors, untie him and take him with you; if you move to a different part of the garden where he will be out of sight, move the tether stake as well.

Always use a harness rather than the collar to tether him: if he suddenly rushes forward or lunges at a passing squirrel it will help prevent neck or spinal damage, and even accidental strangulation. Don't use a long rope or line as this will increase the danger of him getting tangled up in it, and the risk of injury caused by him chasing after something and being brought up hard on reaching the fullest extent of the tether. If he is a large and heavy dog, he may also pull the stake right out of the ground. An ordinary six foot leash will be perfectly adequate.Don't use washing line or similar as this can cut into the skin, and secure him with a quick release knot in case you need to untie him quickly in an emergency.

Clicker training

Some dogs accept the restrictions of a tether without any fuss at all, but others may pull against it. Clicker training can be helpful in teaching him how much more pleasant it will be if the tension on the leash is slack.

Ask him to sit or lie down, and stay close to him at first. Keep quiet if he moves, but as soon as you see any slack in the leash, click to pinpoint the moment and drop a treat on the ground for him, making sure he doesn't have to strain forward to reach it. As he grows more confident, gradually move further away.

This can be a demanding exercise for some dogs, so keep your training sessions short and sweet.

Garden surfaces

Think carefully about what surfaces to choose: as well as the matter of expense, surfaces need to be suitable for your dog (and you), and reasonably easy to maintain.

LAWN

There are lots of benefits to choosing lawn as the main surface in your garden: it absorbs noise as well as pollutants such as carbon dioxide and sulphur dioxide; generates oxygen; plays an important part in temperature regulation, and prevents excess run-off from rainwater. Plus, of course, it's easy on the eye, helping to create a relaxing environment as well as being a nice, reasonably soft surface for you and your dog to play games or lounge around on.

If you have the space, leaving a patch to grow long can benefit wildlife as well as giving your dog a place where he is allowed to graze if he wishes, although make sure you remove seed heads as they form (see *Plants for the garden*).

Lawns aren't always easy to keep looking good

Lawns will suffer from damage more in small gardens and with active dogs. (Courtesy Janet Finlay)

27

when you have a dog, especially an active one, and regularly used areas will inevitably suffer from wear and tear.

If you are considering reseeding or returfing your lawn, choose a grass mixture that is dense and hardwearing so that it stands a chance of surviving, as well as being suitable to local environmental conditions: seed merchants or garden centres should be able to advise you on this. Although seed is an economical choice, remember that you will need to keep your dog off the area until the seed is established, whereas with turf you can both walk on it straightaway, although you should wait until the roots have grown into the underlying soil before making more energetic use of it.

Lawn burns

Unsightly patches of dead, brown grass appearing in areas where your dog has emptied his or her bladder are due to the nitrogen content of the urine. In small quantities, nitrogen is a great fertilizer, but in excess it kills grass. This is why you'll often notice a ring of lush green growth surrounding the dead burnt area, where the nitrogen effect is less concentrated.

Female dogs can be more damaging to lawns than males, not because of any difference in urine, but in toileting habit; they usually squat and empty their bladder in one go, whereas adult males tend to cock a leg and urinate on vertical surfaces, and in multiple locations. Although lawns will suffer less, this can result in plant damage instead. There are a number of products which claim to help prevent lawn burn, but there is little hard science to back this up, or research as regards to safety.

Frequently taking your dog out for walks to relieve himself will help save your lawn's appearance, but probably the easiest method (as well as being safe, cheap and effective) is to leave out a filled watering can. Whenever you see your dog spending a penny, immediately water the spot thoroughly to dilute the urine and, consequently, the nitrogen overload. It will also help prevent the area from becoming smelly in warm weather.

Another solution is to create a special toilet area which you can teach your dog to use. When he goes out in the garden, take him to this place on the leash and wait until he's relieved himself, when you should then praise and reward him, and let him off the leash to have some fun. If you've already taught him a cue word for toileting (see below), this will help. Some dogs learn what's expected of them faster than others: after a week leave him loose and see if he takes himself to the toilet area; if he doesn't, continue to take him there on the leash until the penny drops. If you have a dog flap to allow him to come and go from the garden as he pleases, keep it locked while teaching him to use his toilet area.

Make sure you provide a surface that's acceptable to him, and water it afterward to prevent unpleasant odours. As male dogs prefer a vertical surface to urinate against, install a Pee Post. You can either buy a plastic one, impregnated with pheromones to encourage him to use it, or make your own by hammering a sturdy stake into the ground, and then collecting a small amount of his urine and pouring this over it.

Teaching a toileting cue

Wait until your dog is actually urinating, and then give a quiet verbal cue, such as "hurry up." Praise and reward him once he finishes. He will soon come to associate the cue with the action and relieve himself when asked.

This can be helpful in all sorts of situations, such as before a car journey, or taking him to visit a friend's garden.

Lawn repairs

Urine-burnt areas of lawn may recover if you can teach your dog to leave them alone; give them a helping hand by using a garden fork to make lots of holes and water liberally to dilute excess nitrogen in the area. Repeat this two or three times, then either loosen the surface, mix in some clean soil and re-seed, or cut out the burnt area and replace with a piece of turf. If you grow your own mini-turves in seed trays, these can be used as needed to patch small areas.

Artificial grass

If a real lawn is constantly being damaged by your dog chasing and playing on it, artificial grass can offer a more durable alternative, as well as being very low maintenance. This has come a long way in recent years, and now looks incredibly realistic; it's even available in a range of different 'grass' textures and lengths.

Ali Hetherington has had artificial grass in her garden for the last five years and says of it: "It's great – we do doggy day care and home boarding so it gets a lot of usage in all weathers. In sunny weather it is a little warmer to the touch than real grass, but the sun worshippers seem to love this, and there is always at least one stretched out on it sunning a belly! It's easy to pick up poo from, although does need to be disinfected regularly if you have a lot of traffic on it, as we do, otherwise the smell of wee can hang around in hot weather."

GARDEN SOLUTION

Rachel Jackson and her partner solved the problem of their lawn being unable to cope with wear and tear from their active lurchers by creating a sand garden.

"The grass in the front garden was sparse and the ground became muddy very quickly in wet weather, so we decided to get rid of the lawn altogether. We lifted it up, relocated some of the shrubs that had been growing there, and placed black weed control fabric on top of the soil, pinning it in place. We then covered this with a 6in (16cm) layer of filter sand which is nice and soft for doggy paws. Unfortunately, the fabric got shredded within a few weeks and we had to replace it with a tougher tarpaulin, which has a loose weave that allows water through while keeping weeds from popping up. It's worked really well over the last three years, and only needs a bit of raking occasionally when the sand gets a little untidy and uneven from the dogs racing around on it."

DECKING

Ribbed or grooved boards will help drain water from decking, but this can still become slippery when wet, especially if algae has formed on it, so care should be taken when used in wet weather. Gaps between boards will also help with drainage, but check that if your dog lies down on these that ID discs on collars can't become trapped between them, or paws or toenails when walking across them. If enclosed with a fence, railings should be either close together or wide enough apart that your dog's head can't become stuck between them. Block off any gap beneath the decking if there's any chance he may become wedged should he try to wriggle under it; if there are steps, fill in the risers, as some dogs are frightened by being able to see through the steps and may refuse to walk up them. More importantly, there could be an accident waiting to happen if his paws slide straight off the back of a step.

Chewing

Some dogs love to chew anything wooden; if you spot your dog sinking his teeth into your decking, fencing or garden furniture, divert his attention by giving him something else to exercise his teeth on, and, whilst distracted, spray the area with a taste deterrent such as Bitterapple.

Apart from the annoyance of damage caused by chewing, and the danger to your dog of physical

Grow your own turf repair kit.

If the real thing can't cope with your dog, artificial grass can be an alternative. (Courtesy Ali Hetherington)

29

When Rachel Jackson decided to create a sand garden for her active lurchers, naturally enough they all wanted to join in and help build it. (Courtesy Rachel Jackson)

Decking can look good, but check that it's safe for your dog. (Courtesy Claire Pearson)

injury, supervise a persistent chewer so you can stop him when he tries, because timber used for structures such as decking and fencing has often been treated with preservative (painted on or via pressure treatment) which may be toxic. Use untreated timber if possible, or consider timber substitutes: synthetic materials using a combination of recycled wood and plastic can look good, and be very durable without the need for any possibly harmful preservatives, stains or paints.

GRAVEL

Gravel can be uncomfortable for paws, and so, because some dogs will really dislike it as a surface, you can use this to your advantage by discouraging him from wandering around on flower beds, although it isn't going to be much fun for him if there are large swathes of it in the garden. Small stones may also get stuck to poo when picking it up, which can make disposal more difficult (and will gradually reduce your layer of gravel!).

BARK CHIPS

Bark chips can look decorative and make a good, non-slippery surface for paths, but bear in mind that they will decompose after a while and require topping up. As they rot down, the chips lose their attractive appearance and can make a great habitat for weeds to grow in. As with gravel, pieces can stick to poo when clearing up after your dog, and if he is inclined to nibble on them, they can cause blockages or irritate the gut (see *How does your garden grow?*)

HARD SURFACES

Hard surfacing can be of brick, crazy paving, paving slabs, local stone, mosaic, cobbles, and other materials: contemporary or traditional, there's lots to choose from, with plenty of scope for creativity. Used for pathways, a hard surface will save the lawn from the wear and tear of human feet, although don't expect your dog to follow a path, especially if it's curved as he is more likely to take the most direct route.

Hard surfaces also work well as patio and

barbecue areas, and, as they absorb heat from the sun during the day, often become favourite doggie sunbathing areas.

Avoid playing games on hard surfaces as they are unforgiving if your dog (or you) should fall, and take care in wet or icy weather when they can become slippery.

SLIPPERY SURFACES

Icy weather can make hard surfaces treacherous for both you and your dog to walk on, so encourage him to walk slowly rather than race across them, and use a harness and sling (see *Garden features*) to help support those who need a little assistance due to age or infirmity.

Don't use salt or car de-icer to defrost icy paths as both can be lethal to wildlife and pets: your dog may not lick them directly but is highly likely to lick his paws, which will have picked up traces. If you're worried about venturing out on icy areas, a pair of socks pulled over shoes will give you more traction, or buy a set of grippy overshoes.

Wooden decking can be very slippery when wet: adding anti-slip strips can make it safer, or paint on a non-slip coating.

A build-up of algae can make hard surfaces such as paving, stone flags, and decking very slick: brushing regularly with a stiff brush will prevent the algae from becoming too established, though it's likely that, eventually, you'll need to do more than this. Scrubbing by hand using a stiff brush and plain water will do the job, and, of course, is very safe for your dog, although don't let him drink from your bucket of dirty water. If you want to use a patio cleaner, check the labelling to ensure it is animal-safe, and carefully read any precautions. Many are based on acetic acid – basically vinegar, although more concentrated than the sort you put on your fish and chips. Adding some ordinary domestic vinegar to your cleaning water will help inhibit algae regrowth, although any run-off may kill plants. If using acidic cleaners, try a small test area first, as they may damage the surface of some materials.

If you have a large area to deal with, a pressure

Digging can create havoc in soft surfaces: "Meazy has been digging this hole for six years now – but it keeps him out of mischief and gives him a lot of pleasure, so we don't mind!" says owner Ali Knights. "We fill it with extra soil from time to time, which he takes great delight in redistributing, and have put a Boomer ball right at the bottom to stop him from going too deep." If you would prefer your dog to either dig elsewhere, or to confine this activity to one spot, try constructing a special digging pit: see Enjoying the garden. *(Courtesy Ali Knights)*

31

washer may be more practical and less time-consuming. If you don't want to buy one they can be hired, or you can hire someone to come and do the job for you. Always wear protective goggles and keep your dog safe indoors, especially if he is the sort that likes to play with the jet from a hosepipe when you water the garden.

Should you need to disinfect areas that have been soiled by your dog, use an environmental- and animal-friendly product such as *Safe4*, and after cleaning apply an odour-removing product to reduce the likelihood of that spot being used again.

POO DISPOSAL

Dog poo contains all sorts of nasty bacteria, including *E.coli, Salmonella*, and *Campylobacter*, and it also increases the risk of reinfestation from worm eggs, so don't leave it hanging around in your garden.

Piles of poo will also attract slugs – and if you don't accidentally step in it yourself, your dog might, so if possible pick it up the moment you see your dog produce it, or if not, at least on a daily basis. Sooner rather than later is especially advisable in snowy weather as if left, poo quickly sinks below the surface and is difficult to find again until the weather thaws, when you will have a build-up of soggy messes that are harder to collect.

Poop scooping

You can buy all sorts of poop-scooping gadgets, but the simplest and quickest way to clear up after your dog is to place a plastic bag over your hand like a glove, pick up the poo, and with your other hand pull the bag down over and off your hand and tie a knot in the bag.

Special poo bags are available to buy, including products that are biodegradable or flushable.

Poo disposal

Once you've collected the poo, you have various disposal options:

✿ Take it to a dog poo bin: I have a mini metal dustbin with a securely fitting lid which the poo is placed in, so it's necessary to make only one trip a day to the council poo bin

✿ Flush it: you can flush it down the toilet as long as you haven't picked up stones or garden waste with it which may block the system. And don't flush ordinary plastic bags; if using flushable or biodegradable ones, check first that they are suitable for use in your system

✿ Fit an external disposal unit. If you don't like the idea of carrying dog waste through the house to the toilet, you can buy units which are fitted externally to the existing soil pipe. The poo is placed in it and flushed with water down into the sewerage system

✿ You may be permitted to dispose of it with domestic rubbish: double bag it if you are, but check local authority legislation and regulations as these vary

✿ Install a doggy toilet: these are buried in the garden and bioactivator and water is used to digest waste and flush it into the ground. They should be sited away from vegetable plots, pathways and areas where children play, and are unsuitable for heavy clay soil or where there's a high water table

✿ Set up a wormery: help keep your garden blooming by creating compost from dog poo – but although fine to use on flowers, don't spread it on the veggie patch. The worms in these systems are dog poo-specific, so you can't add plant waste to them

GARDEN SOLUTION

It's possible to build your own poo disposal system, as Deborah Kieboom explains: "We tried several systems but they didn't cope too well with the quantities produced by our dogs – as I also foster Dobermanns, there can be up to four of them around at any one time.

"I use a standard black garden compost bin,

which has an open bottom and stands on bare soil, with a closely-fitting lid to keep the rain out. After I put the dog poo in I always cover it with a layer of sawdust; sometimes, I also add sawdust from the hen coop which has chicken manure in it, and if I can spare it, Bokashi bran. Occasionally, I put nettles or comfrey on top to help the process. There's no liquid seepage, it doesn't smell bad except when I load it up with fresh offerings, and has been working successfully for a year now!"

If you decide to try Deborah's method yourself but don't have hens, substitute dried pelleted chicken manure instead – poultry manure is an excellent compost activator. So is Bokashi bran (a wheat-based material made with micro-organisms and molasses) which is also used to help neutralise smells in wormeries.

Worming
Worms affect all dogs; they can cause gut damage, diarrhoea, dehydration, anaemia, weight loss, stunted growth, and blockages, can increase susceptibility to other diseases, and, in some cases, prove fatal.

People can also be at risk: if *Toxocara canis* eggs are ingested they don't develop into adult worms, but hatch into larvae, which may travel around the body to the lungs, liver and sometimes the eyes, where they can cause impaired or even complete vision loss. Children are especially vulnerable. Picking up promptly after your dog will minimise risk, although you should also teach children to wash their hands after petting or playing with the dog (and do the same yourself). If you have young children you may feel happier if a separate play area is fenced off in the garden where your dog is not allowed, so there is no risk of him fouling in there.

Although picking up poo regularly plays an important part in worm control, it's important to also regularly worm your dog. Wormers only kill the worms present in your dog on that particular day; there is no preventive action to stop your dog becoming reinfested, so initiate a regular programme. Some wormers are not recommended

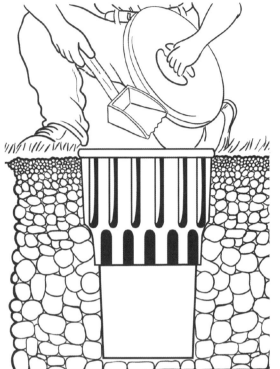

Doggy toilets can be used all year round, although it will take longer for waste to break down in cold weather. A large hole is dug, into which a layer of bricks or large stones is added before placing the toilet in the hole. Regular doses of bioactivator help break down the waste, eliminate smells and repel flying insects, and water is used to 'flush' it. (Courtesy Armitage Pet Care)

for certain breeds, and not all do the same job, so consult your vet about the products most suitable for your dog, and how often he should be wormed.

Coprophagia
Many dogs love to snack on the poo of sheep, cows, horses, or other animals that they come across out on walks; it's normal if rather unpleasant behaviour, and there are numerous theories as to why they do it. It's not normal for him to eat his own poo, however, and can result in health issues. Eating that of cats, birds or other dogs isn't good for him either as it can lead to the transmission of parasites and disease.

If your dog does this, consult a vet who specializes in nutrition as the habit may be due to a dietary deficiency or some kind of digestive problem. If your dog is on a diet it could be that he is hungry, and his meals need to be bulked

33

out with low calorie fibre to give him a full feeling; boredom or copying other dogs may also be underlying causes, or it can be a behaviour he's adopted following punishment for toileting in the wrong place (getting rid of the evidence), or even a compulsive disorder.

Teach a good recall or 'leave it' cue (see *Plants for the garden*) so you can stop him from scoffing any poo he finds; use a muzzle, if necessary; always clear up immediately after him, and, if your vet can find nothing physically wrong with him and all else fails, seek professional help from a behavioural trainer.

GARDEN SOLUTION
Some dogs hate going outside to relieve themselves in bad weather, especially toy breeds and thin-coated dogs who feel the cold. Popping a jacket on can make all the difference.

Don't just turf your dog out into the garden on his own, either, as he'll probably just miserably hang around by the door, waiting for you to let him back in instead of getting on with his business. Wrap up yourself and accompany him so you know he's emptied his bladder or whatever he needs to do; if you're teaching him to use a certain toileting area, you'll also be able to ensure he goes in the right place.

Garden features

The garden is a space that you share with your dog, so you're going to want to have at least a few features for your benefit, but locate these carefully and ensure they're as animal-safe as possible. Although sometimes it's easy to predict what is likely to be a hazard, other dangers may be less obvious: get down onto all fours to gain the same perspective as your dog, as well as visualizing how he is likely to behave. The time of year can also affect things: the steps that are fine in summer can become slippery in wet and icy conditions, while snow can conceal features that your dog may then crash into when running around.

STEPS

Steps may be unavoidable if your garden is on a slope, and whilst they may not present a problem for a fit young dog, as he ages or if he develops mobility issues, it may become necessary to adapt them so that he can cope.

Ideally, steps should be wide enough to allow your dog to stand with all four feet on one step rather than straddling two levels, so it's easy for him to pause if he needs to, and without it causing discomfort. The shallower they are, the better – this is important if you have a small dog, or one with a long back – and preferably wide enough

Steps may be a necessary feature in your garden; shallow risers, wide treads with a grippy surface, and room for you to walk by the side of your dog will make life easier and safer for both of you. (Courtesy www.photographybybenpage.com)

that there is enough room for you to walk alongside him, which will enable you to more easily and safely physically support him if necessary.

An alternative (although this will depend on how steep the gradient is) may be to build a path alongside the steps which your dog may find easier than steps to negotiate. Surface it with bark chips which will be soft underfoot but give better grip than grass when wet or icy.

Wobbly steps are dangerous for you and your dog at any age or level of physical fitness, so repair them sooner rather than later.

If steps have open risers (such as those going up to decking areas might have) fill these in so that paws can't slide through; some dogs find gaps like this very frightening, and may refuse to walk up steps that have them.

Steps constructed with wooden or paved surfaces can be treacherous during wet or icy weather (see also *Garden surfaces*). Applying a weatherproof, slip-resistant finish, fitting textured strips or chicken wire, or covering with non-slip matting will make them safer.

If building steps from scratch, you can, of course, create a safe, non-slip surface by using gravel boards to create each riser, pegging them securely in position, and then backfilling with gravel or bark chips over the top of a weed-suppressing fabric to form each tread (see photo on page 35).

SHEDS
Check that shed doors shut properly and close them after you so your dog can't wander in. Just in case he should get in, though, store tools neatly, with any sharp edges or points turned inward to face the wall. Be especially careful if you keep any chemicals in there, and place them high up on shelves that he can't reach.

After going into the shed, always doublecheck that you haven't accidentally locked him in – small dogs can be easy to miss!

GREENHOUSES AND COLD FRAMES
A greenhouse or cold frame can be really useful for bringing on young plants or protecting tender ones

from harsh weather, but take care that they don't prove to be a liability for your dog.

Broken glass – whether caused by your dog colliding with it, a thrown toy or accidental damage by you – can be razor-sharp, and even more difficult to thoroughly clear up outdoors than indoors. Although stickers or masking tape will create a more visible barrier, my advice is to take further safety precautions: for example, if glazing is of horticultural glass, either replace at least the lower panels with toughened safety glass, clear acrylic panels or polycarbonate sheeting, or cover with glass safety film, which won't stop the glass breaking, but will hold most of the sharp pieces together if it does. Alternatively, you can buy self-assembly, tubular steel greenhouses and cold frames in a variety of sizes and with plastic covers.

Never shut your dog in a greenhouse as he can easily become overheated in there, even when the weather isn't especially hot. If you grow plants which are toxic to dogs (such as tomatoes and aubergines), keep the door shut so there's no risk of him being able to eat them. If you need to open the door for ventilation, either don't grow anything poisonous, fit a secure door guard, or fence off the area to keep your dog right away from danger.

Cold frames can be another hazard; because they are low your dog may not see them until the last minute when running around, and if the lid is left propped open it can slam shut on an inquisitive nose.

DUSTBINS
You might not consider the area where you keep dustbins as being a garden feature, but your dog most certainly will. Decorative, pre-formed bricks or trellis fencing with a gate set in it can be a simple way of screening off the area to prevent your dog from raiding the rubbish, whilst at the same time making it a little more aesthetically-pleasing. If this isn't possible, secure the dustbin lid by sliding a bungee strap through the lid handle and securing the hooks at each end to the handles on the sides to prevent your dog from getting to the rubbish. Quite apart from the mess, he could make

This Stag's Horn Sumach (Rhus typhina) turned out to be one of those serendipitous plantings rather than sensibly thought out and planned, bought at a garden centre after I fell in love with the fuzzy, velvety texture of the new growth of branches. It throws up a lot of suckers which have to be regularly grubbed out, but otherwise it's a real treasure: in autumn the leaves turn vivid yellows and scarlets, while in winter the bare branches have a pleasing architectural structure crowned by deep red, candle-like fruits. But best of all it throws a nice patch of shade right over one of Angel's favourite snoozing spots! Opinion is divided about whether or not it is toxic, so be guided by your knowledge of your dog's behaviour to decide if this is a plant to include in your own garden.

himself seriously ill by snacking on the dustbin's contents.

SHADY AREAS

A shady area can offer a pleasant spot to relax on warmer days, particularly if your garden is a bit of a suntrap. An easy way to create such an area is simply to put up a parasol, which has the added advantage that it can be moved to the most beneficial position as the sun moves. If you want to create a more permanent area of shade – which will also enable you to cultivate a few shade-loving plants – you could fit a canopy, build an arbour, or plant a tree.

An arbour is a fairly instant solution, and there are many DIY kits available to choose from online and at garden and building centres. A tree, of course, is generally a longer-term proposition, and may not cast much shade until it is more mature. When planting, make sure you position it where it will cast shade into your garden, and not that of your neighbour, and remember that if it casts shade over decking or paving, this can give rise to algae forming more rapidly (see also *Garden surfaces*).

COLOUR

Colour can be an important feature in your garden,

Dog-friendly gardening

Garden art can be made from all sorts of things: here, pretty plates hang next to a bottle tree which, on a sunny day, casts deep blue and green reflections on the fence. The origins of bottle trees are as old as the folk tales of imps and djinns captured in bottles and lamps. The idea is that they trap evil spirits inside at night, which are destroyed the next morning by the sun. A dead tree can provide the supports for the bottles, but if you don't have one, try drilling holes in a sturdy stake and inserting lengths of dowel to support the bottles – or even just push broom handles into the ground at different heights and angles and place a bottle on the end of each. If you have a boisterous dog and are worried about using glass bottles, use coloured plastic ones instead.

although more for you than for your dog, who views the world in a more limited range of colours. Flowers and foliage are obviously one way of adding colour, but there are plenty of others, and which will last all year round.

If you have trellis fixed to the fence for annual plants to climb, applying a coat of non-toxic paint will mean the fence doesn't look as bare and dull when annual climbers die back in the autumn.

Pretty plates, bought cheaply secondhand and hung on fences or trellis, make a good substitute for hanging baskets, and won't need any maintenance. Hang them high enough that your dog can't reach them, or if you are worried about having breakable china in the garden, use melamine picnic plates instead.

Give plain terracotta plant pots a makeover with a coat of non-toxic paint; even when they are empty they will still look bright and cheerful, and can do a lot to brighten up a dark area. Make sure they are clean and dry first, and give two coats of paint to ensure good coverage.

Garden art can be a fun way of adding year-round colour to walls and fences; use your own pictures or choose from stock shots which are transferred onto giant outdoor weatherproof canvas. If there are plants you really long to have in your garden, but don't dare risk because of toxicity (or because you have the wrong environmental conditions), this can be a safe way of achieving this.

SCULPTURES

Garden sculptures aren't everyone's cup of tea, but they can add an element of fun as well as provide a focal point. They come in all shapes, sizes, and materials, and in styles ranging from classical to modernistic: if you don't want to buy something, you can always get creative and make your own. If you aren't sure what you want, a visit to a sculpture trail can be inspiring, as well as a fun day out for you and your dog. Do take care in choice and positioning – anything with sharp edges or which may tempt your dog to chew it will need to be placed out of his reach.

WATER FEATURES

Water can be a magnet for some dogs, and you should exercise great care if it's a feature of your garden. A young puppy full of curiosity can drown in a relatively shallow area of water – and even an older dog can get into trouble.

Swimming pools

Swimming pools can be particularly dangerous for dogs of any age, as sheer sides may mean he cannot get out if he falls or jumps in; even though he may be a strong swimmer, once he becomes tired he will sink – dogs cannot tread water or float as we can to conserve energy. Graduated steps at one end may make it possible for larger dogs to escape, but if he falls in and panics, he won't necessarily head toward these, even if he knows they are there. A cover will not necessarily make it safe as your dog may be able to creep beneath.

The only way to be sure he is safeguarded is to securely fence off the area so that he cannot access it. Don't invite your dog to join you in the pool when you are using it, as this may encourage him to jump in when you aren't there.

The chemicals used in the water can also irritate the delicate mucous membranes of his eyes, and cause stomach upsets if swallowed. If your dog loves water, find safer ways for him to have fun – see *Enjoying the garden*. And remember that hot tubs and jacuzzis can be just as dangerous!

Ponds

Ponds can also be a hazard, so think very carefully before installing one. If you do decide to go ahead with this feature, make sure it has gently sloping

Sculptures can provide a focal point. (Courtesy Sally Long)

Some of the deeper inflatable swimming pools can be dangerous for your dog, as Freddie the Italian Volpino found out. A real water lover, even though he is only 12 inches tall and the walls of the pool were 3ft and it was covered, he managed to find his way in, whereupon, of course, he was unable to either touch the bottom, or get out again by himself. Fortunately, he was quickly spotted and rescued. (Courtesy Julii Elliott)

39

*It's easy to create a safe
pond in a pot.*

sides, which will make it easier for your dog to get out in the event of falling or jumping in. It will also make it safer for wildlife, such as hedgehogs, for the same reason.

If it isn't securely fenced off or located in an area your dog doesn't have access to, always keep a vigilant eye on him around the pond. It can be just as unsafe if it freezes over during the winter, when he may be tempted to venture out across the surface. If the ice breaks and he falls through, he could become trapped and unable to escape; he will also very rapidly become hypothermic.

Safe water features

If you have a small garden or are particularly concerned about the safety of your dog around water, you can still have a water feature that is safe. The very safest of all is a dry 'stream,' created by using slate, gravel and cobbles to give the impression of flowing water, which can look very attractive.

If you want real water, a bubble fountain looks good, sounds pleasant, and is easy to install: kits can be purchased from garden and DIY centres. Because the small reservoir of water it uses is concealed below ground level, there's no danger of your dog getting into difficulties, and many love to play with the water as it bubbles up.

Another safe way of having a water feature is to make a pond in a pot: as well as being easy to fit into a small space it is a low maintenance, easy care option.

Choose a frostproof container, and apply several coats of a liquid waterproof sealant to the interior; use a silicon sealant to block any drainage holes in the base. Once this is dry, place a layer of grit in the bottom, and add a few aquatic plants, leaving them in their containers and standing those which need to be closer to the surface on bricks. Add a bunch of oxygenating plants and water, then sit back and enjoy.

If you'd like to watch the play of light on the water's surface, and listen to the sound of running water, a solar-powered fountain should be perfectly adequate for a small feature like this. Moving water

is also less likely to attract mosquitoes, so can have a practical purpose, too.

Do make sure that the feature is safe for birds or other wildlife that may be attracted to it: place large stones or some kind of platform in it so they can get out if they fall in.

Algae

Oxygenating plants will encourage clear, algae-free water, as will plants which float on the surface, filters of the mechanical and biological variety, and using a pump to circulate the water.

Do discourage your dog from drinking from garden water features as even though they may look clear, algae could still be present, and there may also be contamination from wildlife. Ensure he has his own bowl, and that the water in it is replaced daily.

LIGHTING

Strategically-placed lighting in the garden can create a magical atmosphere at night. It can also serve a very practical purpose as it will be much easier to see where you are going in the garden, and allow you to keep an eye on your dog when he goes out last thing. Lights can be reassuring for your dog, too, as not all are confident in the dark. Try to use the minimum amount of nighttime outdoor lighting, however, as a brightly lit garden can disorient moths, bats, owls and other nocturnal creatures. It also disturbs garden birds and can disrupt the breeding, feeding and migration cycles of many nocturnal insects.

Lanterns

Lanterns can be very attractive, but always use with great caution when animals are around. Those lit by candles are safer than those fuelled by oil, paraffin or other inflammable liquids, but still keep them well out of reach of your dog as the lantern will get very hot and can burn a curious nose.

Any naked flame is a risk if your dog is present, so don't use the torch type of garden candle, which is moulded onto a stake and pushed into the ground. Even when cool they can be a hazard:

the candle part can make him ill if he chews on it, while the stake – usually a bamboo cane – can be even more dangerous if it splinters in his mouth and gut.

Electric lights

Any lighting which runs off mains electricity must be installed by a registered electrician; bear in mind that even if they are buried, there is always the chance of your dog exposing cables through digging activities and chewing them (see also *Electricity in the garden* below).

A security light can, however, be a good burglar deterrent, although don't leave it on all night as it can unsettle wildlife, and quite often be annoying for neighbours as well. Install one that is activated by a motion sensor, so that it only stays on for a limited period of time.

Solar lights

Solar lights don't produce as bright a light as electric ones, but are still perfectly adequate to illuminate the edges of paths, beds and other garden features you don't want to trip over in the dark. They are easy to move to different locations, there are no live cables for your dog to chew, and they automatically switch themselves on and off at dusk and dawn. The softer light they produce can be more subtle and relaxing than that of electric light, and is less likely to adversely affect wildlife.

ELECTRICITY IN THE GARDEN

If you have any features in the garden such as lighting or fountains which run off mains electricity, make sure your dog cannot access them. Use toughened cable and bury this underground where it is less likely to be damaged (but note where the cables are). First threading them through a length of hosepipe may give a little additional protection in the event of discovery following digging activity by your dog.

Always get mains-operated features installed by a qualified electrician: they will need to be protected by a RCD (Residual Current Device) – also called a GFCI (Ground Fault Circuit Interruptor), or a GFI in the US and Canada. This is essential to ensure that power is cut off fast enough to prevent a prolonged electrical shock if a fault is detected. Do consider whether you really need such features, or if you could use a safer and more eco-friendly power source instead, such as solar garden lights.

Be very careful when using any electrical equipment in the garden, such as hedge trimmers, strimmers and lawnmowers. Leave your dog indoors so he isn't tempted to chase after and pounce on tempting wiggly cables, or harass the lawnmower (see also *Garden emergencies* chapter).

Heating

Outdoor heating means you can continue to enjoy relaxing in your garden as the weather grows chillier or on cool summer evenings, and chimineas, fire baskets, or some form of garden fireplace can be popular with your dog, too. Many love to snuggle up close – sometimes too close for safety – so use a circular fireguard which will completely surround it, or pop a leash on him to keep him at a sensible distance.

If having a bonfire, it's best to leave your dog indoors, as sparks can fly out into his coat: barbecues are another occasion when your dog may be safer inside (see *Enjoying the garden* chapter).

SEATING

It's nice to have somewhere to sit and relax in comfort in the garden, whether it's a bench that's a permanent feature, or collapsible chairs and loungers which can be put away when not in use. Likewise, your dog will enjoy an outdoor bed of his own, too, which could mean he will be less likely to try out yours.

As he grows older he will especially appreciate a soft surface to lie on that helps cushion ageing skin and joints. A waterproof cover is a good idea in case the ground is damp from dew, or if there is a brief rain shower and you don't have time to take it indoors before it gets wet.

Your dog may have other plans for features originally intended for your benefit ... (Courtesy Sally Long)

ELDERLY DOGS

As your dog grows older, it's likely that his vision and hearing will start to deteriorate, while the onset of arthritis and general infirmity can leave him stiff and unsteady on his feet, and less able to cope with the physical challenges that a garden can present.

Even though your dog is less mobile, and his vision and hearing beginning to fail, there are still plenty of pleasures to be had, albeit gentler ones. He may still enjoy chasing a ball – just don't throw it as far: a stuffed Kong® will be enjoyed, although stuff it a little less tightly: a nap in the sun, or just watching the world go by, or receiving some Tellington-Touch TTouches to help ease aches and pains are just a few of the ways you can continue to enjoy being together outside in the garden.

As your dog ages, you may need to make changes in the garden to enable him to continue to enjoy it. (Courtesy Sarah Fisher)

43

A soft sling can help support wobbly back legs. (Courtesy Sarah Fisher)

44

Mobility

Do ask your vet to check over your dog if you notice he's beginning to have problems coping with slopes and steps, with getting up after lying down, or showing signs of stiffness and generally slowing down. There is no cure for old age, of course, but there are plenty of ways of making him more comfortable; there is absolutely no reason why he should have to endure the pain that arthritis can cause, for example. Many dogs are very stoical and it's only when they receive proper pain relief that you appreciate the discomfort they have been in.

If you have steps, make sure you accompany him, and help him go up and down them, if necessary: a harness can be helpful in supporting the front end, and a sling used to support the back legs. He may also need help rising to his feet after laying down.

Keep lawns trimmed short, as long grass will be more likely to trip him, and provide a comfortable bed for him to snooze on outdoors. As older dogs often sleep more deeply as well as more frequently, be careful not to startle him if you need to wake him: quietly call his name, or if his hearing isn't too sharp, use a smelly treat near his nose to rouse him. Watch that he doesn't overdo the sunbathing as he will be more susceptible to the effects of heat on warm days (see also *Garden emergencies* chapter), and sleeping very soundly, or being reluctant to move due to stiff joints may mean he doesn't seek shade when he should.

Eyesight

Never leave a dog with failing eyesight unsupervised, and if necessary, use a long leash to keep him away from dangerous areas such as steps. A leash can also give him a physical connection to you which may reassure and help him feel more confident.

Even if you have a safe, level area you can leave him to wander loose, still keep an eye on him: make sure obstacles such as plant pots are moved to the sides of the garden so he doesn't bump into them, and that ponds are fenced off or filled in (see also *Water features* on page 39). Be aware, too, that he won't be able to see and avoid any prickly plants and branches in flower beds.

Different textures underfoot will help him orient himself, but you can also use different smells so he can create a scent map in his mind, which will help him find his way around. Use aromatic plants such as Rosemary, Lavender, Garden and Lemon Thyme to help him get his bearings, or mark important areas – such as the door, fenceline, and water bowl – with smells you can place there yourself, although you'll need to remember to keep refreshing these.

Hearing

As his hearing becomes less acute, your dog may not hear when you call him, so be prepared to go and fetch him. If his eyesight is still sound, you could teach him to respond to hand and/or light signals; be careful when approaching him, or rousing him from sleep that you don't startle him, which may cause him to react defensively.

Senility

With age, mental functions can also begin to deteriorate; your dog may become disoriented in familiar surroundings, forget to use his toilet spot, be unable to make it there in time, or even forget what it was he wanted to go outside for once he's there. Be gentle and patient with him: he's not being awkward on purpose.

A deaf dog may not hear when you call him: if he is sleeping soundly, be careful how you rouse him. (Courtesy Corinne Moore/Tina Constance)

Plants for the garden

With plants you can create an interesting environment for your dog as well as yourself: varied forms, colours, textures and scents can transform your garden into a sensory delight.

FLOWERBEDS

What looks good planned out on a sheet of paper may not always be practical in everyday use, so if intending to create new flowerbeds or extend established ones, it can save a lot of work if you first mark out the edges using hosepipe or sand. Leave it like that for a week or so, to give you an idea of how well it fits in with your dog's activities. If you need to alter your plans in light of this, it's easy to do so at this stage!

Keeping dogs off beds

It can be exasperating (and expensive) when plants are constantly damaged or even destroyed by doggy activity in the flowerbeds. Thorny plants may discourage some dogs from pottering around in them, but can pose a risk of injury to eyes and skin, and may be ignored by those with thick coats, or during the heat of the moment if chasing a toy.

Anything but dull – low maintenance heathers and heaths can create a colourful display.

As it is areas of bare soil that are most likely to receive unwanted canine attention – and which are often favoured lounging spots – try not to have any. Plant closely, use ground-covering perennials, or non-organic mulches such as cobbles, pebbles, slate, gravel and shells which will be uncomfortable underfoot for your dog (see also *How does your garden grow?*).

Choose plants that are robust enough to cope with the occasional foray by your dog, temporarily fencing them off while they are young and more vulnerable to damage, so that they have a chance to establish themselves.

PLANTING SUGGESTION

If you have acidic soil, cranberries (*Vaccinium spp*) can make good, low maintenance ground cover plants. In the autumn the berries nestle jewel-like amongst the foliage, and can be used to make your own cranberry relish to accompany the Christmas turkey.

Heathers (*Calluna spp*) and heaths (*Erica spp*) are also easy and relatively trouble-free ground cover plants, which will help smother weeds and provide good shelter for frogs and toads. Although, like cranberries, most prefer acidic soil and a sunny position, there are some which will cope with neutral soils

Teach a 'keep off' cue

If you can teach your dog to stay off your furniture indoors, you can certainly teach him to keep off flowerbeds in the garden in much the same way. If he starts to step onto them, call him away, praising and rewarding him, and with repetition he will eventually get the idea that certain areas are off-limits. You will need to be consistent about this, not letting him wander on one day and insisting that he stays off the next. You'll also need to be careful when throwing toys for him to chase, so that they don't land in a bed, which will create conflict between his desire to go after the toy and his training to stay off that area. Be prepared for his training to only apply while you are actually present in the garden with him: when he is on his

own he may well venture on to the flowerbeds, in the same way as he may make himself comfy on the sofa while you're out! If you want to ensure that he doesn't go on the flowerbeds while you aren't around, either bring him indoors or create a separate run area (see *Living Areas*).

It will make it easier for your dog to determine the boundary between a flowerbed and the rest of the garden if it has a defined edge of some kind. You can buy decorative, pre-formed concrete barriers, use old scaffold boards, bricks

It is possible to teach your dog to keep off beds and borders – but the training may only stick while you are actually around. (Courtesy Will Marsh)

47

set diagonally, or buy mini woven willow hurdles: there's plenty of choice to suit all tastes and budgets.

Green roofs

Not all beds need be at ground level: particularly if planting space is limited, it's possible to create an attractive area of vegetation on the roof tops of garden buildings such as the tool shed, the porch over a door, even dog kennels, bird tables and nest boxes.

Discover some of the benefits – as well as inspiring ideas and practical information – at www.thegreenroofcentre.co.uk and www.livingroofs.org.

CONTAINER GARDENING

There are plenty of benefits to container gardening: if you don't have the right soil conditions for plants you especially want to grow, you can always create them in a pot instead. It also enables you to grow more tender specimens, enjoying them outdoors during the warmer months and moving them into a greenhouse or conservatory as the weather gets chillier.

There are other advantages, too: you can move them around to create a quick garden face-lift, and they can be easier to keep weed-free than beds: by standing one pot on top of another it is easy to create a variety of heights, and as containers come in all shapes, sizes and colours, they can be a decorative feature in their own right (see also *Garden features*).

Container plants will need regular watering during the summer, and unless frostproof may require cold weather protection in the winter. On the plus side the plants won't get trampled on by your dog, and neither will they suffer from having male dogs cock a leg and urinating over them – although you may need to buy tall containers if you have a large dog (see also *Garden surfaces*).

Exposed soil may attract cats to use it as a litter tray, so either keep containers planted up, place a cover over the top, or use an inorganic mulch to prevent this.

It's amazing what you can grow in a pot – not just flowers but vegetables, too, and even fruit. If you want colour as well as produce, try a blueberry plant (*Vaccinium spp*). Easy to grow and fairly resistant to most pests and diseases, prolific small flowers will be followed by a delicious crop of fruit which ripens over a period rather than all at once, and in autumn the foliage of many cultivars (a plant variation within a species which has been selected for specific characteristics, and maintained through cultivation) will turn to stunning flame red and orange hues.

Using vertical space

Particularly if you have a small garden, using vertical space will enable you to keep more of the ground level area free for your dog's use, as well as helping to camouflage fencing. If you want more growing space than your fenceline permits, erecting an archway or obelisk could provide the answer, whilst using the minimum of floorspace.

Fences can also be used to support hanging baskets and other wall-mounted plant containers; these miniature gardens don't need a lot of upkeep so won't eat into precious time you'd rather spend with your dog.

Time-strapped gardeners (or lazy ones) can even buy baskets ready-planted.

Soil left exposed in containers can be a huge unintended attraction for both dogs and cats. (Courtesy Emma Mitchell)

PLANTING SUGGESTION

Nasturtiums (*Tropaeoleum spp*) can be wonderfully versatile as well as easy to grow: set them to climbing up fences, scrambling across beds as ground cover, or trailing from hanging baskets.

Plant support

Some plants need some form of support; if your dog is likely to chew garden canes, use alternatives such as steel ones. Avoid using canes of any type at low levels in case he stakes himself on the top – although yogurt pots placed on the tops will make them more visible, they won't necessarily protect him from injury, and he may remove the pots to play with anyway. Pea netting can also be a hazard as it is all too easy for wildlife, as well as your dog, to become tangled in.

BUYING PLANTS

There are many reputable and helpful internet sites where you can shop for plants, but it's fun to actually go shopping at a garden centre and see what you are buying at first-hand. Joining a local gardening club can be a good idea, as for just a few pounds, membership often entitles you to discounts on products, seeds and plants at various outlets in the area.

Many garden centres allow you to take your dog in, although you should check first, and although the large chains have websites which indicate whether or not your pet is welcome, ring before you go as policy can change, sometimes before web pages are updated. Obviously, you should keep him on a short leash, and toilet him beforehand; on no account leave him in the car, as, even on an overcast day and with the windows cracked open, the interior can become an oven and roast him, while in winter it can rapidly turn into a fridge.

Unless you go with a specific list and exercise a lot of self-discipline, it's likely that as you walk round, at least a few plants will take your fancy which you hadn't perhaps considered. Check labels for advice on toxicity as well as details of height and care; if there isn't enough information to satisfy you, ask staff, and if necessary, don't buy it. Make a note of the plant's name and research it further when you get home, returning to buy it at a later date if it turns out to be suitable.

Car boot sales can often be good sources of reasonably priced plants, too, provided you know what you are looking for, as sellers are not always particularly knowledgeable. Don't rule out pound shops and supermarkets either, as many often offer seeds for sale at bargain prices, as well as garden accessories such as solar lights and hanging baskets.

Get the right one

When selecting plants for the garden, you should buy those that will thrive in the environmental conditions you can offer, obviously, as well as ones that won't pose a hazard to your pet. Where you have either read about, or had a certain plant recommended to you, it's important to check that it is indeed the right one before actually going ahead and buying it. Several different plants may share the same common name – for example, Blacked-eyed Susan could refer to either *Thunbergia alata*, *Rudbeckia hirta* or *Hibiscus trionum* – so establish the scientific Latin name to avoid any confusion.

Seeds

If you have the space and time, growing from seed can be more economical than buying ready-grown plants from a garden centre. There are often more seeds in one packet than you need, and swopping with a friend for some different ones will make your money go even further. Do take care that your dog doesn't get hold of any, though: some can be toxic in themselves, and others because they have been chemically treated.

CHOOSING PLANTS

Choose plants that are suited to your soil type and local environment, and which will do the job you want them to, whether it's producing shade, colour, architectural form, screening or a focal point. Most importantly of all, choose plants that won't be hazardous to your dog.

Acers come in a wide range of shapes and sizes, and many can be grown in containers.

Although toxicity may be your first thought in this respect, many can be troublesome in other ways: sharp thorns or leaves with spiky ends could pierce skin or injure eyes. Some hazards are less immediately obvious; for example, some plants may cause skin irritation – many of the *Tradescantia* species are responsible for contact allergies – whilst ornamental grasses can look beautiful but their seed heads can cause just as much trouble as those of their wild relatives if they become lodged in ears, eyes or nostrils, or work their way in-between toes.

PLANTING SUGGESTION
A tree is definitely something you shouldn't impulse-buy: pick the wrong one and it could become too large for your plot, cast large areas into shade, or have invasive roots. There is a suitable tree for every garden, though, and in this respect it may be worth checking out Japanese maples (*Acer palmatum* species). These have a wide range of different shapes, leaf types, colours, barks and sizes – there are also dwarf varieties suitable for growing in pots, so it's possible to find room for one in even the tiniest of gardens.

Poisonous plants
Plant toxicity can range from mildly irritating to fatal, but much of the information about this is anecdotal and lacking in detail. How dangerous the

plants in question are likely to be can depend on a wide range of factors, such as the dog's age, health status, and the part of the plant eaten, as well as the amount consumed. Just because a dog has been seen to nibble at a plant with no apparent ill-effects doesn't mean that it is safe: non-inclusion in lists of poisonous plants doesn't imply any degree of safety, either, only that there are no known reports of problems. It is probably safe to assume, however, that anything which is stated to be toxic to people will also be toxic to dogs, although the reverse isn't necessarily true.

When deciding what to grow in your garden, it's a case of carrying out your own personal risk assessment: puppies, young dogs, and those which are under-exercised or bored are the most likely to chew or eat your plants, but it's worth bearing in mind that any dog at any age may suddenly develop an appetite for these. It's not just the bits you can see above ground which can be dangerous, either: rhizomes, corms, bulbs and tubers can often be the most toxic part, and bulbs can be especially tempting to dogs if they come across them whilst digging, as they can resemble treats or nuggets of food. Sometimes your dog will pay no attention to a plant while it is growing, but will play with or chew any trimmings or cuttings from it, and in some cases these can be more dangerous when wilting than when alive.

By all means grow toxic plants in your garden (although you might prefer to avoid the more deadly ones) if you are fairly certain that your dog is unlikely to browse on them, but if you don't want to take chances, stick to those plants which are known to be non-toxic.

If you aren't sure what you've got growing in your garden, go take a look with an illustrated reference book in your hand or a knowledgeable friend by your side to help you identify plants. If you are still stuck, try taking a good photograph or a sample along to a local garden centre and ask staff for assistance.

Dogs Trust and the American Society for the Prevention of Cruelty to Animals (ASPCA) both have helpful lists of toxic plants: the ASPCA also

Puppies will chew and nibble at all sorts of things – and not all will grow out of the habit, so you may need to take care which plants you include in the garden. (Courtesy www.photographybybenpage.com)

has a useful picture gallery on its website (see page 54).

Although the plants you choose may be safe for your pet to be around, those of neighbours might not be, and may overhang, or grow through or under fence boundaries, so be sure to keep a regular check on perimeters

Sandy's story
It's not always easy to keep your dog under constant vigilance, and it's invariably during those brief moments when your attention is distracted that problems seem to happen, as Hilda Bootsmann remembers only too well:

"A huge old Yew tree was growing in the garden

❀ Plants to avoid ❀

Common name	Latin name	Comments
Autumn crocus	*Colchicum autumnale*	Also known as Meadow Saffron, Naked Lady
Azalea and Rhododendron	*Rhododendron spp*	Can be fatal
Baby's Breath	*Gypsophila spp*	
Bleeding Heart plant	*Lamprocarpus spectabilis* (formerly *Dicentra spectabilis*)	Also known as Venus' car, Lady's Locket
Bluebell	*Hyacinthoides non-scripta*	Also known as Harebell, Crowbells, Dog leek
Broom	*Cytisus spp*	
Castor oil bush	*Ricinus communis*	Also known as Castor bean plant, African Wonder Tree. Can be fatal
Chamomile	*Anthemis nobilis*	Also known as English chamomile, Roman chamomile
Cherry laurel	*Prunus laurocerasus*	Can be fatal
Christmas Rose	*Helleborus niger*	Also known as Hellebore, Easter Rose
Chrysanthemum	*Chrysanthemum spp*	
Clematis	*Clematis spp*	
Crocus	*Crocus spp*	
Daffodil	*Narcissus spp*	
Delphinium	*Delphinium spp*	Also known as Larkspur, Lark's heel, Knight's Spur. Can be fatal
Dusty Miller	*Jacobaea maritime* (formerly *Senecio cineraria*)	Also known as Silver ragwort
Elephant ears	*Bergenia spp*	Can be fatal

❧ Plants to avoid ❧

Common name	Latin name	Comments
Foxglove	*Digitalis spp*	Also known as Witches' gloves, Dead man's bells. Can be fatal
Honeysuckle	*Lonicera spp*	
Hosta	*Hosta spp*	Also known as Plantain lily
Iris	*Iris spp*	Also known as Flag, Water Flag
Ivy	*Hedera helix*	Also known as Sweetheart ivy, California ivy. Can be fatal
Laburnum	*Laburnum anagyroides*	Also known as Golden Chain. Can be fatal
Lupin	*Lupinus spp*	
Lily of the Valley	*Convallaria majalis*	Can be fatal
Mallow	*Lavatera spp*	
Oleander	*Nerium oleander*	Can be fatal
Pieris	*Pieris japonica*	Also known as Lily of the Valley Bush. Can be fatal
Poppy	*Papaver spp*	
Snowdrops	*Galanthus spp*	
Sweet pea	*Lathyrus odoratus*	Can be fatal
Tulip	*Tulipa spp*	
Winter aconite	*Eranthis spp*	
Wisteria	*Wisteria spp*	
Yew	*Taxus spp*	Can be fatal

Teaching a 'leave it' cue.
(Courtesy Sarah Fisher)

more popular and familiar plants you are likely to find in your garden, and for sale at garden centres and nurseries, which are toxic to dogs, and is in no way exhaustive. You can find more extensive lists and information on the Dogs Trust website www.dogstrust.org.uk and the ASPCA website www.aspca.org.

Teach 'leave it' and 'drop it' cues

Your dog won't know what he is and isn't allowed to eat, chew or play with in the garden until you tell him. If you spot him about to pick up or nibble something you'd rather he left alone, say 'ah ah' to interrupt and distract him, and give him something he is allowed to have, such as a treat or toy. This will also ensure that leaving the object alone is more rewarding for him than ignoring you and continuing to play with it. With many dogs this may be enough, but if it isn't sufficient, spend some time teaching a definite 'leave it' cue.

Offer a low value, rather boring treat in your hand, holding it between finger and thumb with your palm uppermost. Let him take the treat, repeating this half a dozen times.

Next, offer the treat again, but when your dog tries to take it, this time close your fingers around the treat to make a fist, at the same time turning your hand over so the back is uppermost. He may try to get at the treat by pawing at your hand or nosing at it – ignore him and don't let him have it, but don't move your hand away either. Wait until he moves his nose away, then turn your hand palm upward and let him take the treat. Repeat this several times, varying between turning your hand over and withholding the treat, and holding it palm up and letting him have it. Most dogs learn very quickly that a closed hand which has been turned over means they won't get the food, and as soon as this happens you can attach a verbal cue, such as 'Leave' or 'Off.'

It's also a good idea to teach a 'give' cue, just in case he does pick up something and you want him to relinquish it. Do this by first having a brief game with a toy he likes. Stop playing and ask him to surrender the toy in exchange for a really tasty

of our rented house, and, being very aware of the potential danger to my puppy, Sandy, I kept an eye on her all the time she was out there. One afternoon while I was hanging out the washing I turned my back for just a few seconds, and when I looked back at Sandy she was standing beneath the tree and chewing something. I was horrified and immediately called the vet who told us to go to the surgery straight away, and that he hoped Sandy would still be alive when we got there. I have never driven so fast in my life! The vet gave her an injection to induce vomiting, and we then stayed at the surgery for a few hours to make sure everything was fine before returning home. The next day a friend helped me build a fence in the garden to stop Sandy being able to get anywhere near the tree again."

Plants to avoid

The table on pages 52 and 53 lists just a few of the

treat, which you should hold in front of his nose so he can smell it. In order to take it he'll need to let go of the toy in his mouth, so place your other hand beneath his chin, ready to catch it. Keep repeating this until he gives up the toy quickly, at which point attach the verbal cue 'Give.'

If he's the sort of dog who prefers toys to food, offer instead to swap for a higher value toy than the one he has in his mouth.

Keep practising both these skills, as you never know when you might need them!

Poisoning

If you see your dog eating anything which you know is or think may be toxic, or suspect poisoning, contact your vet immediately, as time can be of the essence (see also *Garden emergencies*).

Pet-friendly plants

Although it may seem as if there are many plants to avoid if you own a dog who may be liable to sample them, there are also plenty which are pet-friendly. The table on pages 56 and 57 lists just a small selection of plants which are currently considered by most authorities to be relatively safe, as far as I've been able to determine. Some dogs may, however, be sensitive to some and although not otherwise harmful, they could upset your pet's stomach if he eats them, causing nausea, vomiting and diarrhoea.

New information comes to light all the time, so keep an eye on the internet to stay up-to-date with the latest findings.

FOOD PLANTS

If you have the space – and you don't necessarily need a great deal – it's nice to grow a few edible plants that you can share with your dog, although you will, of course, need to devise a way of preventing him from either helping himself or fouling the crops.

Herbs

It's lovely to have fresh herbs to add to your cooking, but it's best not to grow those destined for the kitchen at ground level, where they can become contaminated by your dog. Keeping them out of reach is easy: you can pack a lot into a hanging basket, grow them on a kitchen windowsill, or in a part of the garden to which he doesn't have access.

Many can also make a decorative or aromatic addition to the garden, or can be added to a 'salad bar' for your dog to nibble at (see pages 59 and 60), including Parsley (*Petroselinum crispum*), Dill (*Anethum graveolens*), Coriander (*Coriandrum sativum*), Mint (*Mentha spicata*), Basil (*Ocimum basilicum*), and Fennel (*Foeniculum vulgare*).

Thoroughly research any herbs you decide to include, as some can be harmful on a long-term basis, or may conflict with any medication your dog is receiving – check with a vet who specialises in herbalism if in doubt.

Although alternative medicine is very popular with many owners these days, don't attempt to medicate your pet (or anyone else's) with homemade herbal remedies. Herbalism can be very effective but it can also be very dangerous, needing careful selection and precise dosage, and it can be easy to underestimate the effects. Leave it to the experts: if you want to pursue holistic treatment, consult a vet who specialises in this modality – attempting to diagnose and treat your pet yourself is illegal and could cause him unnecessary suffering.

Fruit and veg

Fruit and vegetables always seem to taste nicer when you've grown them yourself; they're better for you when eaten fresh, and there are many that you can share with your dog. Be aware, though, that dogs will often help themselves if given the opportunity, and over-indulgence can upset their stomach, so it's best to keep crops out of reach to both prevent this and ensure that he doesn't foul on or near them.

Not all foods which are safe for us to eat are safe for your dog, and some can prove fatal if he eats them. Common offenders include:

continued page 58

❀ Pet-friendly plants ❀

Common name	Latin name	Comments
Alyssum	*Alyssum spp*	
Astilbe	*Astilbe spp*	
Bee balm	*Monarda spp*	Also known as Horsemint
Buddleja	*Buddleja spp*	Also known as Butterfly Bush
Butterfly flower	*Schizanthus spp*	Also known as Poorman's orchid
Calendula	*Calendula officinalis spp*	Also known as Pot Marigold
California lilac	*Ceanothus spp*	
China Aster	*Callistephus chinensis*	Also known as Aster Sinensis
Coneflower	*Echinacea purpurea*	
Coral Bells	*Heuchera sanguinea*	Also known as Heuchera
Cornflower	*Centaurea cyanus*	Also known as Bachelor's Buttons, Bluebottle
Cosmos	*Cosmos spp*	
Deadnettle	*Lamium maculatum*	
Forget-me-not	*Myositis spp*	
Forsythia	*Forsythia spp*	
Giant Aster	*Townsendia sericea*	
Hardy Geranium	*Geranium spp*	Also known as Cranesbill, not to be confused with Geranium (*Pelargonium spp*)
Hen and chicks	*Echeveria spp*	
Houseleek	*Sempervivum spp*	Also known as Stonecrop

❀ Pet-friendly plants ❀

Common name	Latin name	Comments
Impatiens	*Impatiens spp*	Also known as Bizzy Lizzie
Lady's mantle	*Alchemilla mollis*	
Lamb's Ear	*Stachys byzantina*	
Lily	*Lilium spp*	Most are fine for dogs including the related Day Lily (*Hemerocallis spp*) but they are highly toxic to cats, so avoid if you have a cat also
Lilyturf	*Liriope muscari*	
Mahonia	*Mahonia aquifolium*	Also known as Oregon grape
Meadowsweet	*Filipendula ulmaria*	Also known as Kiss-me-quick, Queen of the Meadow
Mosaic plant	*Fittonia argyroneura*	Also known as Nerve Plant
Nasturtium	*Tropaeolum spp*	
Pansy	*Viola spp*	
Petunia	*Petunia spp*	
Phlox	*Phlox spp*	
Red Hot Poker	*Kniphofia spp*	Also known as Torch Lily, Poker Plant
Rose	*Rosa spp*	
Snapdragons	*Antirrhinum spp*	
Sunflower	*Helianthus spp*	
White Ginger	*Hedychium coronarium*	Also known as Butterfly Ginger, Ginger Lily
Zinnia	*Zinnia spp*	

You'll need to find a foolproof way of keeping your dog from raiding the vegetable patch. (Courtesy Claire Pearson)

✿ Grapes/raisins/sultanas can cause kidney failure: just a few can make your dog seriously ill

✿ All of the onion family, including leeks, onions, chives and garlic, as these contain compounds which can cause a form of anaemia, and can be cumulative over time. Although garlic is frequently fed for its anti-parasitic qualities, there is some dispute as to safe levels

✿ Tomato vines, leaves, and green fruit, although fully ripe fruit appears to be relatively safe

✿ Aubergine (eggplant)

✿ Potato plant leaves and stems, and green potatoes

✿ Many fruits contain toxic chemicals in their seeds, stones or pits, including apples, plums, cherries, apricots and peaches. While consuming a few seeds may not be serious, they could be harmful if consumed in quantity, the toxic properties can be cumulative, plus stones and pits accidentally swallowed may cause gut blockages. Other parts of these trees are also toxic, so care should be taken when pruning

❀ Rhubarb leaves

❀ Broccoli has beneficial cancer-fighting properties, but too much can do more harm than good: if intake exceeds 10 per cent of your dog's diet it can cause painful stomach upsets, while in excess of 25 per cent it can be fatal

PLANTING SUGGESTION
Strawberries can work well in hanging baskets; combine with pansies or violas to provide colour as the strawberry flowers fade, or add trailing nasturtiums for a touch of extra drama – their flowers and leaves can also be added to salads, making them practical as well as pretty.

Why do dogs eat grass?

No-one really knows the answer to this often-asked question, although there are plenty of theories. Some dogs appear to enjoy it more than others, and on the whole it doesn't seem to do any harm, beyond occasionally causing them to vomit, due to their digestive systems not really being cut out to deal with quantities of long, coarse fibre. Today, most dogs don't get enough of these important nutrients in their food and it can affect their mood, their blood chemistry, and skin health.

Leaving a patch of grass to grow long will allow your dog to browse if he wants to – and is safer for him than grazing while out on walks when foliage may contain poisonous weeds or have been chemically treated. Alternatively, plant up some containers with a bit of greenery to which your dog can help himself. Overleaf, Angel is enjoying nibbling at her own personal salad bar which includes pots sown with ryegrass from a box of garden lawn seed, oats (*Avena sativa*) – often sold in packets in pet shops as well as garden centres as 'Cat grass' – parsley (*Petroselinum crispum*), and American Land Cress (*Barbarea verna*). Purists had better look away now as there is also a pot of couch grass (*Elytrigia repens*), also known as

The brilliant early blooming colours of Lungwort (Pulmonaria officinalis) also known as Spotted Dog, are a wonderful indicator that spring really is on its way. Great gapfillers, these also have a long tradition of being used in herbal medicine, although if your dog is a nibbler, they're best avoided.

Dogs are often very partial to fruit, but it's not always safe to let them help themselves. Gather any windfalls before he does, and so that they don't attract wasps.

twitch or dog grass: a gardener's enemy, perhaps, but much enjoyed by the dogs, and not a problem when safely contained in a pot.

A doggy salad bar like this doesn't need much attention, but as the grasses mature, seedheads will form, which should be trimmed off so they

Meazy checks out 'his' ginkgo tree. (Courtesy Ali Knights)

cannot become lodged in ears, eyes or noses, or irritate or penetrate the gut if swallowed. Resow regularly, too, so your dog has a choice of young, sweet stems and older, more fibrous stalks.

NEW PLANTS IN THE GARDEN

Anything new in the garden – including plants – is likely to capture the interest of your dog, and if he is too enthusiastic in checking them out, they may suffer as a result. Temporarily fencing off an area containing young plants or seedlings, and protecting young trees will give them a chance to become established and better able to withstand his attentions later.

Ali Knights still remembers her dismay when her Miniature English Bull Terrier, Meazy, discovered the exciting new tree she had bought for the garden: "I had saved up some birthday money to buy a Ginkgo, and on a visit to a garden centre, found just what I wanted – two-and-a-half feet tall with a perfect 'ball' head, and looking like a golden lollipop. It was a vast amount of money: more than I'd ever spent on a plant for the garden, so I transported it home with great care. When I got

back I immediately unloaded it and then let Meazy into the garden while I went to fetch the container and compost I'd also bought so I could repot it. As I reached the side gate with these, I saw to my horror that Meazy was merrily cavorting round the garden with my precious Ginkgo. During the scuffle that followed to get it off him, the beautiful golden globe of foliage – already only hanging on by a thread where Meazy had partially bitten through the stem – finally parted company with it completely. Once repotted, Meazy lost interest in it, and amazingly (and following helpful advice from the lady at the garden centre), it not only recovered but is thriving, although the round ball is these days more of a diamond shape ..."

TOOL SAFETY

Try to be a tidy gardener while tending your plants: many tools can be dangerous if left lying around – for you as well as your dog should either of you trip over or stand on them. Always keep your dog indoors when using machinery such as hedgetrimmers, strimmers and lawn mowers.

How does your garden grow?

Nourishing your plants and eliminating pests and weeds will contribute to a flourishing garden, but the methods you use need to be safe for your animals, as well as effective.

Organic v chemical gardening

Lots of chemical products offer a quick fix, but before you rush off to buy any, it's worth pausing for a moment to consider if they're really necessary: very often there's a chemical-free alternative. Working with nature may take a little longer to provide results, and require a little more effort from you, but does have plenty of benefits:

❁ You'll be helping wildlife: chemicals can spread through the food chain and affect species other than the ones you want to eliminate. Many pesticides aren't pest-specific anyway, so you can end up killing all the useful bugs as well. Wiping out whole populations of insects will also deprive their natural predators of food that may be essential to their survival – ladybirds can't exist without aphids to feed on; slugs and snails are an important part of the diet of thrushes and hedgehogs, while blue tits need to collect around 10,000 insects to feed a brood of babies

❁ Helping the environment generally: artificial pesticides, weedkillers and fertilizers are energy-intensive to produce. Some may also be slow to break down, lingering long after they've been used or are wanted

❁ The garden will be a safer place for your dog: no matter how 'pet-friendly' a product may claim to be, if the labelling tells you to wash your hands after contact with it, to wear protective gloves or clothing when using it, or to avoid inhaling or ingesting it, I'm always inclined to regard the claim with a degree of scepticism

Using chemical products

If you do buy commercial chemical products, always read the small print and instructions for use very carefully. They may only be 'pet-safe' when diluted, or used in exactly the way directed. Many may require watering in, and that pets are kept away from treated areas for a certain period of time, and can still have the potential to make your dog ill if he chews on a pack of it.

Going organic

Adopting an organic approach to gardening is about achieving balance and working in harmony with nature, rather than trying to force it into submission – aiming for control rather than eradication.

Obviously, it also helps if you choose healthy and disease-resistant plants suited to soil type and location, as they'll be more likely to thrive without the need for chemical assistance. You should also be aware that although organic techniques can be safer for your dog, they aren't necessarily hazard-free, .

Compost heaps

Compost is a terrific way of improving soil structure, helping it to retain moisture and nourishing your plants. If you have the room, making your own is cheaper than buying it, and the perfect way of recycling old bedding plants, lawn mowings, newspapers, egg cartons, and uncooked organic kitchen waste. If garden space is limited, or you don't generate sufficient quantities of waste and kitchen scraps for a compost heap, you can still create compost (and a useful liquid fertiliser) by using a small wormery instead.

You can either make your own compost heap container or buy a compost bin; local council recycling initiatives may mean you can buy one at a discounted rate. Whether home-made or purchased, it's important that it's dog-proof, so you can keep him from rummaging around in it and snacking on anything inappropriate. Rats can also be a problem: although ideally your compost heap should sit on bare soil, we had to place ours on paving slabs and use wire mesh around the base to prevent rats from tunnelling and chewing their way in. The bottom was lined with newspaper and some old compost to absorb liquid run-off, and this seems to have done the trick.

Don't add cooked foods, meat or fish (raw or uncooked) as this will attract your dog as well as vermin; it's best not to put stones and pits from avocadoes, apricots, peaches, nectarines and cherries in either. These are toxic to dogs and are unlikely to have rotted down by the time your compost is ready to use. Dog faeces shouldn't be added: although it is possible to compost them, this should be done separately (see *Garden surfaces*).

If possible, turning your heap occasionally will discourage rodents from setting up home in there, but wear a face mask and keep your dog away while doing this due to the risk of Aspergillosis. This can be extremely unpleasant for your dog, is difficult to treat, and can permanently damage the lining and bony structures of the nasal cavities. The presence of microscopic *Aspergillus* fungal organisms is also another good reason for not allowing your dog to snuffle round the compost heap.

Mulches

Mulches laid on the soil surface can help suppress weeds, conserve water, protect from winter frost, and enhance the appearance of a flowerbed. Some can also deter certain pests, and – if uncomfortable to walk on – may discourage your dog from digging or playing in flowerbeds.

You can use organic substances including

compost, bark chips, newspaper, cardboard and dried grass clippings, or inorganic materials such as gravel, pebbles, cobbles, seashells and coloured glass pebbles. Inorganic mulches tend to be expensive but long lasting; organic ones will rot down in time and need to be topped up – although this does have benefits in that it will improve soil quality.

Some mulches can also affect soil ph, so you

Make sure compost heaps can't be accessed by your dog.

63

Inorganic mulches that feel uncomfortable underfoot will help discourage your dog from walking across areas you'd rather he didn't.

may need to check this occasionally, or if your plants begin to look a little peaky.

Although they can be beneficial for your garden, not all mulches are good news for your dog. If you have one that likes to pick up and play with stones, avoid pebbles, cobbles and glass beads, and when selecting inorganic mulches, pick those which have rounded rather than sharp edges that will cut paws if walked on.

Never use cocoa shell mulch: this looks good and smells as delicious to dogs as it does to us, with the result that your dog may be tempted to eat it, with potentially fatal consequences. A by-product of the chocolate industry, the hulls contain theobromine, a chemical that dogs are especially sensitive to, and which can lead to the same symptoms as with chocolate poisoning. Spent hops, another by-product, can also be a popular mulch, but is also toxic to dogs.

Coconut fibre mulches are also best avoided if there is any risk at all of your dog ingesting them, as they can absorb up to ten times their own weight of water and will swell in the gut, causing a blockage. Coir briquettes are small, light and easy to store compared with other compost products, but can be equally dangerous if your dog gets hold of one and decides it's fun to chew on.

Not all wood bark or chip products may be suitable, either: the antifungal and flea and tick repelling properties of cedar make it attractive to dog owners, but concerns about its safety have been expressed. The essential oils and resins it contains can cause skin irritations in some animals, and if ingested, may cause vomiting and drooling.

The same applies to pine and spruce, whilst *any* wood mulch can cause gut blockages. Pine needles can be great for areas around acid-loving plants, but not so good if they penetrate the skin between toes and pads, or the mouth and gut; rubber chips are long lasting but could be lethal if eaten. Although it may seem unlikely, it doesn't mean your dog might not try to eat any of the foregoing: there really is no accounting for some of the things that dogs might put in their mouths and swallow.

Choose untreated products, check the packaging to see if it says 'non-toxic' or 'safe for pets,' and contact the manufacturer for more detailed information if necessary. Tree surgeons can be a source of free wood chip mulch, but check that it's not from toxic plants.

Weed control

Try to keep on top of weeding: done regularly, it's less of a chore and ensures weeds don't get a chance to flower, set seed and multiply. Annual weeds such as chickweed, groundsel, shepherd's purse, hairy bittercress and annual meadowgrass are fairly easy to deal with, using either a hoe or hand fork. Perennials such as stinging nettles, bindweed, couch grass, ground elder and docks can be tougher customers, and need to be dug out; if you chop them off at ground level or leave even a tiny piece of root behind they'll regrow. When hoeing, pay attention to areas which look bare as well as where you can actually see weeds, so you also destroy those weeds that are germinating.

Annual weeds can be added to your compost heap or – if you have hoed and the weather is dry and sunny – left on the soil's surface to wither and die. Perennials can be incredibly persistent, so dispose of them by either burning or drowning in a container of water. Once rotted they can be safely added to the compost heap without worrying that they'll regrow.

Membranes and mulches

Once you've cleared your beds of weeds, laying a fabric membrane can be an effective way of suppressing regrowth – unless you have a dog who likes to dig, in which case it can be a disaster! The amount of devastation that can be caused by it being 'discovered' and dragged out can be almost unbelievable. You can, of course, give him his own special area to excavate, and teach a 'keep off' cue (see *Enjoying the garden*, and *Plants for the garden*), but while setting this up, using either a deep layer of mulch or a thinner one laid over sheets of wetted cardboard or newspaper may be a more sensible idea (see previous section).

This Creeping Speedwell (Veronica peduncularis) provides great ground cover – every year in late spring/early summer it is a mass of glorious blue flowers, and even bounces back from Angel occasionally deciding to lounge about on it. As it can smother other plants as well as weeds – a lone orange flower of a Geum can be seen as it sinks from view – you may need to keep it in check.

Planting

Planting densely and using groundcover can be another way of helping to choke back annual weeds – plus, of course, it looks nice, provides shelter for frogs, and makes flowerbeds less inviting to neighbourhood cats who may regard exposed soil as the perfect toilet area. Be careful in your plant choice, though, so you don't end up replacing an invasive weed with an equally invasive plant.

Feeding your plants

One of the best ways of keeping plants healthy and well nourished is to get composting (see page 62). This will minimise the need for additional feeding with fertilisers, but if you really feel these are necessary, and decide to use a commercial product, choose with great care and read thoroughly all of the instructions and precautions for use on the packaging. Fertilisers which are combined with herbicides and pesticides are best avoided altogether.

While many fertilisers are relatively safe when used as instructed, they can sometimes cause problems if ingested, so be sure to keep packets and containers well out of reach of your animals. Products which contain hoof, blood, bone and fishmeal may also prove irresistible to dogs, encouraging them to dig and even eat the soil or anything else they uncover, such as toxic bulbs and corms. Liquid fertilisers are often preferable to those in pelleted forms, which may be mistaken for treats.

Dogs and animals who come into contact with recently fertilized areas may develop a skin irritation, or the product can be accidentally ingested when the paws or coat are licked.

When it comes to home-made alternatives, you must be equally cautious. Coffee grounds are often suggested as an organic fertilizer suitable for acid-loving plants (and as a slug-repelling barrier), but are highly toxic to dogs if ingested. Manure or manure tea (made by soaking a bag of manure in water) may not be a great idea if your dog is likely to roll in it or eat it (or both). It can, however, be a brilliant way of kick-starting a compost heap, and a valuable addition to it thereafter. By the time the heap has rotted down and is ready to use, it will have turned into a lovely rich mix without the same aromatic attraction for your pet.

Another favourite do-it-yourself feed is comfrey tea, but there is a question mark over its safety, as this herb has been linked with cancer and liver damage when ingested. You can make a useful feed in the same way using nettles instead: chop them up, place in a bucket and weight them with a brick. Add enough water to cover and leave to steep. As they can get a bit smelly, cover with a lid and leave to brew in a remote corner of the garden. After three or four weeks the solution should be ready to use – dilute first by adding ten parts of water to each one of nettle tea. The sludgy foliage left over can be added to the compost heap.

A wormery will also produce a rich liquid feed, and is a good way of recycling uncooked organic kitchen scraps if you don't have room for (or don't want) a compost heap.

Your dog may consider a patch of bare soil perfect for sunbathing on, but before long weeds will pop up and begin to take over. Buy him a comfy bed and mulch or plant some groundcover there instead.

Pest control

It can be disheartening to see carefully nurtured plants being ravaged by pests, but pesticides are likely to be just as unwelcome in your garden if you have a pet and care about wildlife. Many commercial products are highly toxic to dogs, and kill off beneficial bugs as well as bad ones. Even those which are pet-safe can be equally indiscriminate, but when the pests return (and they will), the natural predators you exterminated at the same time won't be around any more to help keep them in check, leaving you locked into a cycle of chemical dependence.

Rather than trying to beat nature, get it to work for you instead. Choosing plants which are low on the pest attraction scale can be a place to start, and there are plenty of other things you can do which aren't reliant on chemicals. Some of these are discussed in this chapter; it's likely that you'll need to adopt more than one strategy.

NUMBER ONE GARDEN ENEMY
The 'bad' guys you're likely to find in your garden include aphids, caterpillars, ants, scale insects, and vine weevils, but it's usually slugs and snails that top the list of problem pests. Consequently, the shelves at garden centres are often sagging under the weight of anti-slug and snail products. Some of these can be fatal to dogs, and even the 'safer' alternatives aren't entirely risk-free.

Popular anti-slug and snail killers include products based on:

✿ Metaldehyde and methiocarb: these can kill if consumed by pets – added taste and smell aversives don't necessarily deter them. Methiocarb is also an insecticide, so will kill helpful as well as unwanted bugs, including beetles that prey on slugs. Birds and hedgehogs

Right: Slugs and snails can pose a health risk to your dog as well as be a pest in the garden.

may also be harmed by eating the pellets, or the poisoned slugs

✿ Aluminium sulphate: can irritate eyes, skin and the respiratory system if inhaled; bad news for fish if it gets into ponds, and there may be links with Alzheimer's disease (which dogs can also be affected by, although in them it's called Canine Cognitive Dysfunction)

✿ Iron phosphate: iron poisoning can cause damage to the digestive system, liver and heart, and although a lot may need to be eaten to do damage, you don't want to experiment on your pet to find out just how much proves fatal. Small quantities ingested over a period of time can be cumulative, as dogs cannot excrete excess from their bodies

Slug and snail health risks

As well as munching their way through your plants, slugs and snails can be carriers of a life-threatening parasite called *Angiostrongylus vasorum*, also known as Lungworm or French heartworm.

Infection occurs when an infected slug or snail is eaten: even if your dog doesn't do this intentionally, they can be accidentally swallowed while eating grass, or if stuck to a toy which has been left in the garden. Infection can also occur via larvae in slime trails being ingested.

Symptoms include coughing, lethargy, depression, weight loss, vomiting, diarrhoea, nose bleed, weakness, seizures, paralysis, and persistent bleeding from even minor cuts. Early treatment will lead to full recovery, but left undiagnosed and untreated, the condition can be fatal. Not all wormers are effective against this parasite, so consult your vet if you think your pet is infected or at risk. Poop scooping, both in your garden and out on walks, plays a part in preventing transmission.

ENCOURAGE NATURAL PREDATORS

A pest to you may represent a good meal for its natural predator, so it's worthwhile encouraging wildlife in the garden.

A bug's life

Entice beneficial insects into your garden and they'll rid it of vast numbers of pests. Adult ladybirds and lacewings and their larvae will gobble up aphids, as will hoverfly larvae; ground beetles will feast on caterpillars, leatherjackets, vine weevil and slugs, while centipedes will eat a variety of insects and small slugs. Even those who aren't predators can still play a helpful role in your garden: for example, woodlice and millipedes help to aerate the soil and break down organic matter.

Wasps can also be a good gardening ally as they feed their young with caterpillars and insect larvae, and help with pollination, but if your dog can't resist snapping at them and is likely to get stung, you may prefer to do without them. Rather than killing them, try discouraging them by using a Waspinator (see *Garden emergencies*).

Plants that will attract beneficial insects

There are plenty of plants to pick from which will

A ladybird – one of the good guys.

69

attract a variety of beneficial insects – you might even consider leaving a few dandelions (*Taraxacum officinale*) in the lawn, but more conventional choices include those in the table on page 71.

Nematodes

If you need extra help tackling garden pests, you can buy species-specific nematodes. These pet- and wildlife-friendly microscopic predators make their way into their host's body where they release a bacteria which ultimately results in its death. The nematodes produce a second generation which seeks out other hosts; when there are no longer enough to support them, they die off themselves.

Shield bugs

If your dog encounters a shield insect – also known as chust or stink bugs – while sniffing around the garden, it may not be a meeting he'll enjoy. These bugs produce a fine mist of foul-smelling liquid to deter predators, which can irritate the skin and cause burning to the eyes. If this happens, flush with clean water and seek veterinary advice.

Make an insect hotel

Providing winter accommodation for beneficial insects will mean increased numbers in your garden the following year, ready to wage war on your pests. A pile of logs in a secluded corner is an easy way to do this, and you may find frogs and toads sheltering there, too. If space is limited, buy or make a 'bug hotel' instead: a very simple one can be constructed by cutting the end off a large plastic drinks bottle, inserting a roll of corrugated cardboard or bamboo canes cut to length, and then stuffing round the edges with scrunched up newspaper or straw to hold it in place and provide insulation. Use string to hang it vertically, open end downward so it doesn't fill with rainwater, and set it up before the end of summer so hibernating insects have time to move in.

Strictly for the birds

Birds can be a great form of bug control: blackbirds, thrushes, robins, starlings, rooks,

Right: If you're a leggy blonde, a birdtable is perfect for those in-between meal snacks! After being caught red-pawed, it has now been relocated somewhere that Tallulah can't help herself. (Courtesy Anne Whitfield)

❀ Plants to attract insects ❀

Common name	Latin name	Comments
Basket of Gold	*Aurinia saxatilis*	Also known as Golden Alyssum, Gold-dust
Blue scabious	*Leucospermum incisum*	Also known as Pincushion flower
Canterbury bells	*Campanula medium*	
Coneflower	*Echinacea purpurea*	
Coreopsis	*Coreopsis*	Also known as Tickseed
Coriander	*Coriandrum sativum*	
Dill	*Anethum graveolens*	
Fennel	*Foeniculum vulgare*	
Lemon balm	*Melissa officinalis*	
Marigolds	*Tagetes spp*	
Parsley	*Petroselinum crispum*	
Poached egg plant	*Limnanthes douglasii*	
Pot marigold	*Calendula officinalis*	
Spearmint	*Mentha spicata*	
Spike speedwell	*Veronica spicata*	
Stonecrop	*Sedum album*	
Sunflower	*Helianthus spp*	
Sweet alyssum	*Lobularia maritima*	
Zinnia	*Zinnia*	

crows and jays will help keep down slugs, while tits, wrens and goldcrests will eat aphids. Aphids are also popular with many seedeaters, such as chaffinches, green finches and goldfinches, who feed them to their young. Supplementing their diet during the winter will ensure plenty of regular feathered visitors who will gobble up garden pests during the warmer months; you can buy various mixes according to the type of birds you want to encourage. Be aware, though, that dogs can often be just as predatory as cats, and may chase, catch and kill garden birds. Putting a bell on his collar can help reduce the number of fatalities; falconry bells are expensive but have a clear, reasonably loud sound, and will jingle at the smallest movement.

PLANTING SUGGESTION

Once you've enjoyed the show, the seeds of sunflowers (*Helianthus*) can provide a great high-energy source of food for birds. If you're not keen on giant varieties, there are plenty of dwarf cultivars which will look great in beds or containers.

Prickly visitors

Hedgehogs can also be useful garden pest controllers, but if you want to put out food to encourage them to return, never offer bread and milk as this will make them ill. Cat food (but not a fishy variety), a good quality, high meat content

Help hedgehogs to help you fight garden pests by adopting wildlife-friendly practices, and keeping your dog out of their way.

wet dog food, dried mealworms, or the special hedgehog food sold in some garden centres and pet shops are all suitable. Once the hedgehog has moved on, remove any leftover food so that it doesn't encourage slugs or rats – or provide an unintentional snack for your dog.

Hedgehog numbers have declined considerably since the 1950s, so any help you can give is welcome, and that includes ensuring they aren't harmed by your pet. There seems to be something about hedgehogs which dogs can't abide; apart from badgers, they are the only other animals which regularly injure and often kill them, so if you know (or suspect) that one visits your garden, keep your dog under control on a leash when he goes out in the evening until you know the coast is clear. It isn't just large dogs who will attack hogs – small ones can be just as belligerent in this respect.

Hedgehogs often fall victim to certain gardening practices, too: keep drain openings covered so that they can't fall in and then not be able to get out; avoid using netting which they can get tangled up in, and always check under piles of leaves and bonfires in the autumn before setting fire to them, as they may conceal hibernating hedgehogs. Take care if turning a compost heap, too, since these can also be preferred over-wintering sites. Ponds can be dangerous if they fall in and the sides are too sheer to climb out (see *Garden features* for advice on creating safe water features). Leaving an opening of 4in (10cm) in your fence at each side will allow hedgehogs to come and go freely – although this may equally apply to young puppies and small dog breeds, and may encourage diggers and chewers, so use your discretion as to whether this is a sensible option. Lastly, take care when strimming and mowing, as very many hogs are injured – often fatally – when these applicances are being used.

Pond life

Frogs and toads will eat slugs, beetles, spiders and caterpillars; the best way of encouraging them into your garden is to provide some kind of water feature. This can be a very simple, shallow affair

Frogs will eat plenty of garden pests.

and doesn't need to be deep, so shouldn't pose a hazard to your dog. Cool, dark shelter such as an upturned flower pot or a few rocks or logs arranged together, with a patch of longer grass around the edges, will make your garden an even more inviting place.

Toads can sometimes cause problems if your dog licks or tries to pick one up, as they secrete a foul-tasting substance through their skin as a form of self-defence. Although this may cause him to foam at the mouth and appear distressed, in the UK it is unlikely to result in anything worse than an unpleasant experience. Flush out his mouth with plenty of water, keeping his head pointing downward so the water runs out and not down his throat; if at all concerned, seek veterinary attention.

In other parts of the world some species can be deadly, and direct contact may not even be necessary as venom may be left behind on food or water bowls they've sat on. In such areas, accompany your dog if he goes out in the garden at night when they are most active: if he does come into contact with the venom, rinse out his mouth and take him to the vet straight away.

Collect snails at night by hand, and check empty pots as these are favourite hiding places for them to shelter in during the day, and hibernate in over the winter.

PLANT DETERRENTS

While some plants attract beneficial insects and predators, others have a reputation for deterring pests. Many herbs, including Coriander (*Coriandrum sativum*), Dill (*Anethum graveolens*) and Fennel (*Foeniculum vulgare*), can be worth growing for their repelling as well as their culinary qualities, and can be dotted through flower beds. If you want colour as well, Petunias (*Petunia spp*) are said to repel aphids and leafhoppers, and Calendula (*Calendula spp*) to repel aphids. You'll find other suggestions opposite under *Smellpower*.

PLANTING SUGGESTION

Mint (*Mentha spp*) is allegedly effective against mice, but as it can be very invasive, contain it in a pot which you can either place on top of, or sink into the soil.

PATROL THE BORDERS

Go out into the garden with your dog last thing at night, taking a torch with you, and while he's pottering around having a last pee before bedtime, you can be doing a little pest control. Slugs, snails and vine weevils are most active when it's dark, and you can find and collect them by hand, disposing of them as you see fit and according to your level of squeamishness. If you release rather than kill slugs and snails, make sure it's at least 100 metres away as they have a homing instinct and will otherwise head straight back.

Check the borders during daytime, too, shaking flowers and the branches of shrubs to dislodge snoozing earwigs; knock out container grown plants and check for vine weevil larvae, and lift upturned pots, stones and other dark or shady hiding places favoured by slugs and snails, taking care to replace so as not to deprive a frog or toad of a home. Deal with aphids by using a jet of water on the plant concerned; ensure you do the undersides of leaves, but take care not to damage fragile blooms.

MAKE TRAPS

Put up with earwigs if you can, as they eat aphids and other small prey and their eggs; but if you can't, trap them in flowerpots packed loosely with hay or straw and placed on the tops of canes staked amongst your flowers, and in 12in (30cm) lengths of old hosepipe laid on the ground. Check and empty these each morning, but relocate your prisoners rather than kill them.

Vine weevils will hide out in rolls of corrugated cardboard during the day, while slugs will seek out dark, damp places. Cabbage leaves and the skins of halved, squeezed oranges and grapefruit will attract them, and you can then easily find and dispose of them.

Beer-baited traps will attract slugs; they can also attract dogs, who may view them as a new and novel treat dispenser. Alcohol is not good for canines, and neither are beer-marinated slugs, come to that, so make or buy traps with lids that will keep doggy noses out.

BARRIERS

Barriers can also help protect plants against slug and snail attack, although they are only effective against those on the surface and outside of the barrier.

Slugs and snails dislike moving across dry and/or scratchy surfaces, so sharp grit around vulnerable plants may help deter them (it will also inhibit vine weevils from laying eggs), or make protective pot collars from the used sandpaper of orbital sanders or leftover scraps of roofing felt. Crushed eggshell or crushed oyster shell can be used, too, although not near acid-loving plants as they will make the soil more alkaline.

As discussed earlier, 'non-toxic' granules and powders may not be ideal when dogs are around as they may walk over, sniff at, or lick them.

Copper will deter slugs and snails as they receive a small electric shock when they come into contact with it. Products include copper rings, self-adhesive tape for pots, impregnated fabric, and even a resin that can be applied to a variety of surfaces. You can make your own copper rings for plants in beds by applying the tape to sections of plastic drinks bottles.

Tree guards, either bought or made yourself

from wire mesh or plastic drinks bottles, will help protect against voles, rabbits and deer.

SMELLPOWER

The power of scent can be harnessed to discourage many pests and unwelcome visitors:

✿ Ants: cinnamon, cloves, cayenne powder, curry powder. They also dislike growing Lavender (*Lavendula spp*) plants and those of the Mint family (*Mentha spp*)

✿ Aphids: Fennel (*Foeniculum vulgare*), Marigold (*Tagetes spp*), Nasturtium (*Tropaeolum spp*)

✿ Cats: vinegar – soak wads of paper and position in places they frequent, lion poo (can be bought in pelleted form from garden centres), citrus peel (if squeezed orange and grapefruit halves are left out they will double as slug traps)

✿ Deer: hang sweaty T-shirts round the perimeter of the garden

✿ Moles: orange peel

✿ Rabbits: lavender (*Lavendula spp*), thyme (*Thymus spp*), garlic (*Allium sativum*), but take care when using garlic-based sprays or products. Although less toxic than onions, if eaten in excess garlic can cause anaemia, and as many dogs seem to enjoy the smell and taste, it may also lead them to seek out and graze on plants they would normally ignore

✿ Rats and mice: peppermint oil

✿ Slugs: Rosemary (*Rosmarinus officinalis*)

✿ Squirrels: fox urine (can be obtained as a powder from garden centres, although there is a danger that your dog might find it fascinating

PLANTING SUGGESTION

The grey-green foliage of the 'Scaredy Cat Plant'

It can be difficult to discourage cats from coming into your garden, and you may need to experiment with different methods to find which works best on your particular feline interloper. (Courtesy Corinne Moore)

(*Plectranthus caninus* or *Coleus canina*) produces a strong smell which many cats (and dogs) dislike. Easy to propagate, try growing it in pots which you can move around until you find the best place.

CATS

Even if your dog lives harmoniously with your cat, other felines may be a different matter, and are liable to be chased. If caught, it may be seriously injured or even killed; your dog is also unlikely to escape unscathed in such a conflict (see *Garden emergencies*).

It can be very difficult to keep cats out of gardens, and even though they know dogs are present, and may have tangled with them previously, they can be persistent trespassers.

There are many methods you can try to discourage them; how effective they are depends on the individual, so you may need to experiment.

These include:

✿ Scent deterrents: various products are available from garden centres, and can be sprayed around the perimeter of the garden (see also page 75)

✿ Water pistol: relies on you spotting the cat and being within range. Will probably continue to visit when you aren't around in any case

✿ Motion-activated sprinkler: can work well, but only when the cat is within range; switch off when your dog is in the garden

✿ Cover bare soil: use ground cover plants or pebble and cobble mulches to prevent flowerbeds being used as a feline restroom

✿ Ultrasonic deterrents: these may be motion-activated or hand-held; your dog may find them unpleasant, too, so they should be switched off when he is in the garden

❀ Models: birds of prey, fake snakes and cats with staring glass eyes – need to be regularly repositioned

FLEAS AND TICKS

As well as plant pests, you may encounter fleas and ticks deposited in the garden by wildlife, or picked up by your dog on a walk and brought home. As well as causing intense irritation and often triggering skin allergies, fleas can carry tapeworm, while ticks can transmit Lyme disease – to you as well as your dog. Preventive products in the form of sprays and spot-ons are available, but if you prefer to follow a chemical-free approach, *Steinernema carpocapsae* and *Steinernema feltiae* nematodes can help control flea and tick populations in the garden.

You should also inspect your dog daily for signs of these parasites. As it's possible for your dog to have fleas without you actually seeing one, check his coat for flea dirt by holding a piece of damp white paper near the base of his tail while you brush briskly, flicking all debris and dust onto it. Any that dissolves leaving a reddish smudge is flea dirt – lots of anti-flea methods and products are available, so ask your vet about which is the most suitable to use on your pet.

Ticks can be tiny – sometimes less than 1mm – so aren't always easy to spot, and can be mistaken for warts. If you don't use chemical preventives, use a tick hook to safely remove it, checking that the mouthparts have come out, too. It is important not to squeeze the body or stress it by applying oils, alcohol or petroleum jelly, as this can cause it to regurgitate its stomach contents into the bloodstream, increasing the risk of infection. You can find out more about ticks and tick-borne diseases at www.bada-uk.org.

RATS

Rats can make wonderful pets, but wild ones roaming in your garden can pose a serious health risk to you and your dog. Discourage them by removing any sources of food – put out only enough food for the day on birdtables, and don't leave grub out for your dog. Don't add cooked or other foods to the compost heap that will attract them, turn it regularly and, if necessary, buy a composting unit which they can't access (see also *How does your garden grow?*).

If rats do take up residence, call in pest control which will be able to advise on other measures to take. Rodenticides are one of the most common causes of poisoning in pets and wildlife, and can be fatal, whether ingested directly, or indirectly through eating a rodent that has been poisoned, so are best avoided if possible.

The alternative is to use traps. When using the lethal sort it is essential these are placed where your pet cannot reach them with a paw or nose. If you opt for a live capture trap, you will then have the dilemma of what to do with the rat: disposing of it humanely may be difficult, and although brown rats can legally be released in the UK, legislation varies in other countries.

When weighing up the pros and cons of various methods of rodent control, you'll find some helpful information on the Universities Federation for Animal Welfare (UFAW) site at www.ufaw.org.uk/rodents.

Rachel Jackson's rescued Podenco cross, Bandit, loves to mooch around in the garden, one of his favourite places being a pathway between some bushes and the fenceline. One evening a mysterious lump was found on Bandit's shoulder, which, on closer inspection, turned out to be a tick. Shrubberies and long-grassed areas can be favourite spots for ticks to lie in wait for their next free meal, so carefully check your dog each day. (Courtesy Rachel Jackson)

Enjoying the garden

The garden is a place which offers lots of different opportunities for you and your dog to interact, as well as for pursuing your own particular interests.

SUNBATHING

Not everything you use your garden for has to be active or challenging; sometimes it's nice just to simply relax. Sunbathing is a favourite pastime for many dogs, although some have little sense about when they have had enough, and you may need to gently persuade them to move into the shade. Remember that, even then, it can still be very hot, and that humid weather can make it difficult for your dog to lose heat effectively (see *Garden emergencies*).

A bed or dog hammock will make sunbathing all the more enjoyable.

Right: A hosepipe or sprinkler can provide plenty of entertainment for water-lovers. (Courtesy Sally Long)

GETTING WET

Some dogs adore water, and a paddling pool can be fun and cooling in warm weather.

The rigid, plastic shell-type children's paddling pool/sandpit are sturdy, and won't be punctured by your dog's toenails, as will an inflatable one, but put a rubber bath mat in the bottom so that he doesn't slip. If you prefer, you can buy larger,

purpose-made canvas pools that don't need inflating. Add some interest and encouragement for dogs who are a little unsure about getting their feet wet by tossing in a few toys and treats that will float.

Some dogs also love to play with the water from a hosepipe or sprinkler, so watering the garden can also be an opportunity to have a game with him; don't direct the hose or sprinkler straight into his face, and if the hosepipe has a nozzle, adjust it to produce a gentle spray rather than a powerful jet of water. Never turn a hose on a dog who is frightened of it or water, or throw him into a paddling pool.

SNOW BUSINESS

A fall of snow can transform your garden into a new and exciting environment for your dog. It can also conceal features such as steps and pots which may cause injury to your dog if he collides with them, so be careful where you throw snowballs for him to chase after. Snow can also ball up between his

A paddling pool can be the perfect way for your dog to have fun in warm weather. (Courtesy Maria Johnston)

If you both wrap up when it's cold, you can carry on having fun in the garden.

79

Be careful when playing throwing games, as your dog will have his eye on the toy rather than where he's going.

quantities of cold snow or ice could cause painful stomach cramps. As newly-fallen snow is around 90 per cent air, and only around 10 per cent moisture, it's a poor substitute for water if your dog is thirsty, so be sure to keep his bowl topped up with a fresh supply.

Winter time blues

It's thought that, as with people, some dogs are affected by Seasonal Affective Disorder (SAD) during the winter months, exhibiting similar symptoms to human sufferers, such as being less active, sleeping more frequently and for longer periods, and showing an increased interest in food.

SAD is thought to be linked to seasonal changes in light affecting the production of certain neurotransmitters, which play a part in regulating sleep, mood and appetite. During the winter your dog is likely to be spending more time indoors, and if you work, may have to go out for his walks while it's dark, so will be getting less exposure to sunlight. If you can't take your dog for his main walk during daylight hours, maybe you could arrange for a dogwalker to do this for you; try to keep up his exercise anyway, as physical activity helps boost serotonin levels and a feel-good response. And, of course, carry on spending time in the garden at weekends – unless conditions are extreme, you can both wrap up warmly and continue to play games or have short training sessions outside.

If you do notice behavioural or physical changes in your dog, do get him checked over by your vet as although mood changes may appear to be seasonal, they could also be related to underlying health problems. Don't rule out the possibility that you might be projecting your own feelings onto him if you suffer from the winter blues: dogs are highly sensitive to our moods and yours could simply be picking up on this.

PLAYING GAMES

Playing games with your dog is an important bonding activity as well as a fun way of interacting with him, and the garden offers lots of scope for

toes and pads, which can be painful and affect his stability, so before going out apply some Musher's Secret, a wax-based protection for paws (http://musherssecret.net/). Cold conditions can be as challenging for some dogs as high temperatures, with very young or elderly dogs and those with thin coats being particularly susceptible.

Go and have some fun together in the garden, by all means, but don't spend too long out there, and pop a jacket on your dog first.

Many dogs will bite at and eat snow as well as try and pick up snowballs thrown for them; provided it is clean and uncontaminated, this shouldn't cause any harm. All things in moderation, however: if excessive amounts are consumed it can lower the core body temperature, making your dog more susceptible to hypothermia. If he is hot (after energetic exercise, for example) eating large this. You will need to be careful when it comes to throwing games, as even though you may have taught your pet to stay off flowerbeds, in the heat and excitement of the chase he may blunder straight into them, undoing your training.

His acceleration can also be surprisingly fast, and is often considerably better than his braking powers, or he may be so focused on the toy he is pursuing that he fails to notice obstacles in his path, as Toni Shelbourne discovered:

"My dog, Buzz, was a lively terrier cross who loved chasing after his rubber Kong® toy. While playing with it in my parents' garden one day, it bounced off the ground, ricocheted off a boat trailer parked next to the shed, and carried on in a different direction. Unfortunately, Buzz was already on course to catch it on the trajectory it had been on moments before, and he collided face-on with the metal rim of a wheel. The result was four chipped incisors in his lower jaw and a sore mouth; I was mortified by what had happened.

"It wasn't the end of the story either, as years later those same four teeth had to be removed when they started to rot and cause problems."

Children and dogs

It can be fantastic for children to grow up with a family dog, but always, always supervise interaction between them, no matter how placid and tolerant your dog, or gentle and well-behaved your child usually is.

The picture right was taken when Hayley Price's daughter, Evie, was 11 months old: "Ziggy – with the help of TTouch – had coped very well with the introduction of a baby into his home, but this was the first real time he had interacted with her. There's nothing Ziggy likes more than to chase a ball up and down the garden and, despite the fact that he has a very gentle nature, we kept a very close eye on them both as Evie learned how to throw a ball for him. We needn't have worried as they both behaved perfectly!"

Toy safety
Encourage your pet to play with appropriate, safe

toys which are sufficiently sturdy and robust, and never leave him alone with anything that can be chewed up or ripped apart in case he swallows pieces (which won't necessarily pass safely through his system), or chokes.

Never throw or allow your dog to chew on sticks, whether it's one collected while out on a walk or retrieved from the garden. Apart from possible toxicity issues, splinters can become stuck in the mouth, pieces swallowed, and life-threatening throat injuries caused. Visit www.colliecorner.com/stick-to-toys to read some heart-rending true stories if you need convincing further.

FOOD IN THE GARDEN
The garden can be the perfect place to make meals last longer and satisfy the scavenging urge in dogs: if your pet bolts his food, needs a little more mental stimulation, or is on a diet, try scattering a handful of kibble on the ground which he'll have to work harder for, instead of presenting it to him in a bowl.

Toys such as balls and pyramids which contain food are often better outdoors, too, as there is more room to bat them around, and they won't get wedged behind or under the furniture. A well-stuffed Kong® will provide quieter entertainment when you want your dog to be a little calmer, as well as an outlet for legitimate chewing activity. Check that any toys with hollow cavities which can be packed with treats have at least two holes,

Josie and Loki are the best of friends. (Courtesy Matthew Stokey)

Evie and Ziggy learn how to play together. (Courtesy Hayley Price)

Even the best of friends can fall out over coveted resources such as toys and food, so keep a careful eye on them, and be ready to step in before trouble starts.

plug the small hole with a dab of peanut butter or cream cheese, then sit the Kong® in a yoghurt carton or similar so that it stays upright while you fill it. Begin by putting in a base of crushed dog biscuits, then add a layer of low- or fat-free fruit yoghurt. Pop some fruit in, such as a slice of banana, a few raspberries, a strawberry or some blueberries, then top up with more yoghurt and finish with another piece of fruit on top of that. Place the Kong®, still in the carton, in the freezer until frozen. If giving to your dog straight from the freezer, run the Kong® briefly under the tap first to ensure the outside isn't so cold that his tongue gets stuck to it.

If you prefer, you can make a mini cheesecake instead in the same way, using an empty, individual-size yoghurt carton as a mould, and turning it out before giving to your dog. As these treats can be a little messy on carpet, the garden really is the best place for your dog to enjoy them!

Barbecues

It's not only your dog who enjoys eating al fresco – during the summer it can be fun to invite friends and family round for a barbecue. Sometimes it's better if your pet keeps a low profile indoors on such occasions, as the cooking area can be dangerous for him, and for the chef, too, if he gets underfoot.

Even the best-mannered dog in the world may assume that the normal rules don't apply to mealtimes out of doors and succumb to temptation, either begging for or stealing food. Seasoned and marinaded foods could upset his tummy whilst some, such as onions, are toxic; if he gets hold of meat skewers, cooked bones or corncobs, these could prove fatal. Drinks, as well as plates, are often placed on the ground where they can all too easily be accessed by your dog; alcoholic or caffeinated beverages are toxic to dogs and can kill.

Even if your pet is perfectly behaved, guests may be less well-trained, and unable to resist slipping him unsuitable titbits, so you'll have no idea what or how much he's eaten. With lots of

otherwise the tongue can create a vacuum inside, causing it to swell and lead to injury. Don't leave food toys out when your dog isn't actively playing with them, as they will attract vermin, and in warm weather flies as well. Pick them up, remove any food your dog hasn't eaten and wash thoroughly.

As food is a valuable resource for most dogs, be very careful if children are around when your dog has it: make sure they know not to go near the dog and, if they are too young to understand, give your pet his treat in a separate area where he won't be disturbed. If you have more than one dog, even though they are normally the best of friends, they may fall out over food, so should be carefully supervised. Place them in separate areas to enjoy food-stuffed toys if there is any risk of a dispute breaking out over possession.

Cool Kong® recipe

A frozen cheesecake-style Kong® makes a delicious cool treat for your dog on a warm day. Temporarily

Toys containing food are usually popular!

Dog-friendly gardening

Even the best behaved of pets will find it hard to resist a barbecue. (Courtesy Claire Pearson)

Cookie gets busy in her new digging pit. (Courtesy Sarah Fisher)

people coming and going, there is also a danger of him escaping if a gate or door is accidentally left open.

If you really can't bear to leave him out of the gathering, put him on a leash and in the charge of someone responsible. Prepare a small pot of safe treats which anyone wanting to give him something can dip into.

DIGGING PIT

Not all dogs dig, but if you own one who does, it needn't be a problem.

If he is digging in order to escape or because he's bored, then you'll need to address these issues – see also *Safety and fencing* in *Keeping your dog safe*. Some dogs will dig to create a cool bed to lie in during warm weather, or may be copying you as you cultivate beds, while others (especially terriers) simply love to dig!

It's usually more successful to redirect digging activities – which are, after all, a fairly natural doggy behaviour – than to try and stop them entirely: prevent excavation in one spot and it'll probably just happen in another.

Create a special digging pit, if possible locating it in the area where your dog has been concentrating most of his previous activity. How big it is depends on how much space you can spare, but if possible, dimensions which are twice as long as your dog in width and length will give him plenty of room. If you aren't very good at DIY, buying a raised bed kit is a quick and easy way to construct the edges; once you have sited it, use a garden fork to loosen the top layer of soil very slightly, and top up with clean top soil. Some people use sand, which can be irritating to certain dogs, and although small amounts may pass through his system okay, larger quantities can cause stomach

Try hiding a few treats or a favourite toy to make a ball pit even more exciting. (Courtesy Sarah Fisher)

upsets, constipation, and even impaction, which may require surgery. If your dog is accustomed to digging in soil, he may also prefer it to sand.

Don't use spent compost from containers, or any bought compost that may have been chemically treated. Make a lid from a sheet of hardboard or waterproof tarpaulin so you can cover the pit when not in use to prevent cats from using it as a litter tray.

Encourage your dog to use his special pit by burying treats and toys in there for him to find. As well as varying the locations, hide them at different depths, too. You can also place treats on the surface, but make them harder to access by covering with a flower pot which can be partially pushed into the soil. He might not realise they are there at first so call him over and show him, by digging yourself using fingers or a trowel, as well as giving verbal encouragement to get him started.

Don't tell him off if you find him digging anywhere else; simply interrupt the behaviour and direct him to his special digging area.

Pica

The habit of eating non-food items such as sand or soil is called 'pica,' and can be due to a number of causes, including nutrient deficiency, lack of bulk or fibre in the diet, and boredom. It can also be a compulsive behaviour in some dogs, but the first course of action you should take is to consult your vet.

Sometimes dogs become obsessed with playing with small stones and pebbles, and will accidentally swallow them. As well as causing blockages in the gut this practice also carries the risk of damage to teeth, and should not be encouraged. Provide a selection of more appropriate toys, including some which are good to chew.

Tunnels aren't just for
terriers!

BALL PIT

A ball pit isn't just for kids – dogs can have really good fun in them, too! Use a rigid plastic clam shell – or even an inflatable children's paddling pool as it won't matter if claws pierce the bottom – to contain the balls, and throw in a few tasty treats for him to find. You can make an alternative version of this for next to nothing by filling a large cardboard box with scrunched up balls of newspaper and popping in a few treats.

TUNNELS

Many dogs will enjoy running in and out of a tunnel – buy one which is sturdy enough that toenails won't penetrate the fabric, and which can be stabilised so it doesn't roll around as this could scare more nervous dogs.

AGILITY EQUIPMENT

Agility is an activity that combines elements of obedience and athleticism, and will really hone both your own and your dog's powers of observation and communication. As well as being good exercise it's also a great form of mental stimulation which requires your dog to use his brain. Even in a small garden it's usually possible to set up one or two agility obstacles that you can vary from day to day to keep it fresh for him. You can buy equipment from online suppliers which folds up for easy storage when not in use, or make your own. It's essential for the safety as well as confidence of your dog that you introduce and know how to use it safely, so it's a good idea to join an agility club (see *Contacts and resources*), and have some lessons together before practicing at home.

PROBLEM-SOLVING GAMES

There's a whole range of special problem-solving games which involve using nose or paws to manipulate moving parts of a toy in order to retrieve a treat. As well as being ultimately rewarding for your dog when he succeeds in getting the treat, these encourage him to use his brain to work out how to get it.

You can also make your own problem-solving games: pop a treat inside an eggbox, or if that's too easy, inside the cardboard inner tube of a kitchen towel, twisting both ends of it so that the treat doesn't fall out. Place a treat underneath a towel (the bigger the towel, the more difficult it is) or roll it up, swiss roll- style, inside the towel for him to unwrap. An excellent reference for games that can be played in the garden and indoors is *Dog Games – stimulating play to entertain your dog and you*, published by Hubble and Hattie.

The flower pot game

This is another popular brain game you can play with your dog, which is a favourite with Maxine

Problem-solving games give your dog a mental workout as well as helping improve dexterity and co-ordination. (Courtesy Sally Long)

87

Romeo demonstrates the flower pot game. (Courtesy Kynos Verlag)

very food-orientated, and his reward for finding it will be a quick game with it instead."

PARTY ANIMALS

Your garden can be the perfect place to hold a doggy party; maybe a celebration of your pet's birthday or 'gotcha' day – or for no other reason than to get together with friends and have fun.

A successful garden party will need a little careful planning in advance. Begin by drawing up an invitation list, but invite no more than you can comfortably accommodate in the space you have available, and choose well-behaved guests (both two- and four-legged) who will get on together. Provide party food for dogs as well as people, but make sure everything is clearly labelled to avoid any confusion about what is intended for whom.

Don't forget to put out plenty of water bowls, and to keep an eye on them during the party in case they need refilling. Finally, before your guests arrive, remember to hang out poo bags with directions to a bin where used ones can be deposited.

It can be a good idea to get proceedings under way by all going for a walk first, so arrange for everyone to meet up at a certain time at a suitable venue such as a local park. This will give the dogs a chance to meet each other on neutral ground, and have a good run to let off any excess energy before heading back to your house. It also ensures that they've had plenty of opportunity to empty bladders and bowels.

You may already have permanent or temporary features set up to amuse your canine guests such as a play tunnel, digging pit, a paddling pool or ball pit, but organising a few games can be fun for everyone, and help things go with a swing.

Have a variety of games which need different skills so everyone gets a chance to shine, such as:

❀ Bonio-and-spoon race – like an egg-and-spoon race but using a dog biscuit instead of an egg. The handler holds the spoon and biscuit (use small spoons to make it extra difficult) in the same hand as the dog's leash

Bray's three dogs, Red, Teale and Ikna. It can be a good way of starting nose work with young puppies, and is great mental stimulation for dogs of any age, which taps into natural instincts.

Maxine explains: "Set out half a dozen flower pots, upside down and with a strong-smelling treat under one of them. Put your dog on the leash and encourage him to sniff at each of the pots and to knock over the one which has the treat under it. Let him eat it and give lots of praise, too. Most dogs get the idea after a few goes, and you can move the pots further apart and let him off the leash, telling him to 'find it' using an enthusiastic voice. As he gets better at it, start hiding them under bushes or behind plant containers to make it harder for him to find them – and do it while he isn't watching you, too!

Don't hide the pots within flowerbeds if you are going to train him to stay off them, though, as it will be confusing if you suddenly change the rules. You can use a favourite toy in place of a treat if he isn't

❀ Musical sits – the doggy version of musical chairs. Scatter mats or sheets of newspaper on the ground to substitute for chairs

❀ Sausage bobbing – provide buckets of water with a piece of frankfurter floating on the surface. If you feel that owners ought to participate too, set up separate buckets with apples in them

❀ Obstacle race – set up a variety of obstacles, some of which have to be completed by the owner, and some by the dog (and maybe some by both). Fastest clear round is the winner – make sure you have a stopwatch ready

Watch out for any potential clashes between dogs, especially where food is involved, and choose some slower paced, more calming games if anyone – dog or owner – begins to get over-excited!

BUBBLE MACHINE
Yes, you can even buy battery-operated machines which will produce a stream of bubbles for your dog to chase and try to catch. They don't appeal to all dogs, but for those who do like them they can provide plenty of entertainment, especially if you buy the special chicken- and beef-flavoured bubble mixtures.

You can also buy water pistol-style bubblemakers – or just make your own by twisting a piece of wire into a circle with a handle, which you can either blow through or wave around to produce bubbles.

TELLINGTON-TOUCH
Creating some peaceful and tranquil associations with the garden for your dog will teach him that it isn't a place just to run and jump, but where he can also settle and relax. Doing a few of the special Tellington-Touch 'TTouches' can be a good way of achieving this; it's also a lovely way of spending some quality time with an older dog who can't participate as actively in games, or if he needs to take things easy following surgery or illness. As

a bonus, you'll also find that TTouches can be as soothing and enjoyable for you to give as for him to receive.

Tellington-Touch was devised by Linda Tellington-Jones: the special ways in which the skin, limbs and tail are moved influence the nervous system, and can produce dramatic beneficial effects. As well as a general 'feel good' factor which can help in forming a bond between animal and owner, TTouches can reassure, promote calmness and confidence, and even help alleviate some of the aches and pains of age or injury.

When doing the TTouches, contain your dog gently but don't pin him down. If he doesn't like what you're doing, try using a lighter pressure, a faster or slower speed, placing a towel over him and doing the TTouches over the top of it, working on a different part of the body, or a different TTouch. Concentrating on what you're doing can make you stiff and tense, making the TTouches feel

Try blowing bubbles for your dog to chase as a change from balls.

89

Tellington-Touch can be a good way of helping your dog to relax and settle outdoors. (Courtesy Sarah Fisher)

unpleasant, so relax, enjoy what you're doing, and remember to breathe! Doing the TTouches slowly tends to calm, while doing them faster is inclined to stimulate.

If your dog is nervous, restless or excited and you want to calm him, you may need to start off fast, gradually slowing down as he accepts the TTouch. Many dogs love ear work – you can find out how to do this on page 110, *Garden emergencies*.

Here are two other simple TTouches you can try.

ZIGZAGS

This is a good introductory TTouch. It's also great for:

❀ Warming up your dog before exercise and cooling down afterward

❀ Dogs who are sensitive to being touched and may dislike being petted

❀ Dogs who don't like being groomed

❀ Gaining the attention of nervous and hyper dogs

❀ Dogs who freeze on the spot when on the leash

Zigzags 1

(Courtesy Sarah Fisher)

Zigzags 2

(Courtesy Sarah Fisher)

Llama TTouch. (Courtesy Val Borland)

1) Stand or crouch next to your dog while he is standing, sitting, or lying down . Rest your fingers on his shoulder and move your hand downward along the muscle, allowing your fingers to spread apart as you do so.

2) As your hand comes back up toward the spine, allow the fingers to loosely close together again. Keep the pressure light, but firm enough that you don't tickle.

3) Change the angle of your hand slightly each time you complete an upward or downward movement so that your hand travels along the length of your dog's body and over the hindquarters in a zigzag pattern. When you've done one side, do the other side as well.

LLAMA TTOUCH

Llama TTouches are very soothing and calming, so are useful for dogs who are:

❀ Timid or nervous

❀ Anxious about being touched on certain parts of the body

Use the whole length of the backs of your fingers, from the tips to the furthest knuckles.

Working over a 'confidence course' can produce lots of benefits. (Courtesy Sarah Fisher)

Gently and slowly stroke along the side of your dog's muzzle, along his head, body and down the legs, keeping your fingers slightly curved so they are nice and soft.

If your dog shows concern about you touching certain parts of his body, move your hand to a place where he is less anxious, and when he relaxes try gradually approaching the difficult area again. Remember that this may indicate the presence of a physical problem, so ask your vet to check him over if you suspect this may be the case.

As well as stroking with the backs of your fingers, you can also try making circular movements in preparation for other TTouches: lightly and gently move the skin as you do so, rather than sliding over the coat.

TELLINGTON-TOUCH CONFIDENCE COURSE

Setting out a 'confidence course' of obstacles for your dog isn't so much about testing his athleticism as about helping him improve his co-ordination, balance, concentration, self-control and co-operation. As these skills develop, you'll see all sorts of everyday benefits, be it his ability to walk without tugging on the leash, or in overcoming motion sickness in the car. You can also walk him round a confidence course in the garden to help him learn how to disregard people passing by on the other side of the fence – although don't ask the impossible too early; position your obstacles as far away as possible before gradually moving them closer as he learns to cope with each situation.

You don't need any special equipment – look around the house and garden and use what you have to hand, including different surfaces such as plastic, cardboard, plastic trays, door mats, rubber bath mats, carpet tiles and cushions, plus low poles to step over, a ladder laid flat on the ground so he can step in and out of the rungs, and old bicycle tyres laid flat. Upturned flower pots or plastic bottles filled with water to weight them can make great slalom markers to weave in and out of; crush drink cans in the centre to make supports for raised poles.

Take your dog through the course on a leash; it's not a race, so don't rush but ask him to walk slowly, and to stop and pause as he puts his feet on each new surface.

TRAINING – USE IT OR LOSE IT!

Training is for life, and doesn't stop when you finish a class: if you don't keep it up on a daily basis your dog's responses will deteriorate. The garden can be a great place to train your dog, offering more space and scope for exercises such as recall and walking nicely on the leash. It's also a good transitional area when building up distraction levels, as there'll be more to divert him than when indoors, but less than when out on walks. As well as brushing up on basic obedience, add a touch of variety by teaching a few tricks, or an activity such as agility or Treibball (http://www.treibball.co.uk).

GOING VISITING

Before visiting anyone else's garden with your dog, check that he'll be welcome, and ensure he has been well exercised beforehand and had a chance to empty his bladder and bowels.

Don't let him off the leash until you are sure there are no hazards or poisonous plants, and remember that just because you find certain behaviours acceptable it doesn't mean other

Anita Janssen's dog, Spotty, demonstrates her Treibball skills, showing that it's possible to do all sorts of things in even the smallest of garden spaces. If your dog loves balls, or is a herding breed, this can be a really fun game to play together which provides plenty of mental stimulation. (Courtesy Anita Janssen)

93

Before going visiting, make sure your dog has been well exercised, and introduce him to your host's dog on neutral ground. (Courtesy Janet Finlay)

people do, too, although they may be too polite to mention it. Be ready to scoop any poo your dog produces, and if he starts to dig, run through flowerbeds, or behave in any way that is unacceptable, pop him back on the leash again.

If your host also has a dog, don't assume they'll be fine: introduce (or re-acquaint) them on neutral ground away from the house, by taking them for a short walk together. Your dog may also be a welcome visitor at parkland and landscape gardens, but do observe any requests to keep him on the leash – usually meaning a short, fixed-length one rather than an extending one at full stretch.

Visit Hubble and Hattie on the web: www.hubblrandhattie.com and www.hubbleandhattie • blogspot.com
f twitter • *Details of all books • Special offers • Newsletter • New book news •*

The indoor garden

Although you might not regard it as such, it's likely that you also have an indoor garden of sorts – even if it only consists of keeping a few herbs in the kitchen for cooking, or a bunch of cut flowers to brighten a room. Houses with conservatories attached offer even more scope as an indoor garden area, where you can bring tender plants in from the garden during the colder months of the year, or grow more exotic specimens.

There's no doubt that house plants can be beneficial to both humans and pets. The ancient Chinese tradition of Feng Shui believes that they can help circulate positive energy forces within the house, and create a more harmonious environment. If you prefer hard science to mysticism, NASA research has shown that house plants can do a huge amount to remove toxins and improve air quality.

There are also definite psychological effects: those who are ill appear to recover more quickly when plants are present, whilst brightly-coloured examples stimulate the release of endorphins and adrenaline, giving an energy boost and providing a feel-good factor. Although dogs may be less affected by colours than humans, they will, of course, still benefit from *your* more upbeat mood.

As with outdoor plants, household plants can pose hazards of which you should be aware. A dog left on his own indoors while you are out may become bored, and more inclined to check out any flowers and foliage, not all of which are safe.

HOUSE PLANTS

You might have chosen a house plant for its attractive appearance or pleasant scent, but your dog may be more interested in finding out if it's good to eat, or maybe play with. If you catch him trying to browse, use your 'leave it' cue (see

Cut flowers create an instant splash of colour round the house – but choose with care.

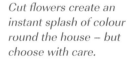

95

Plants for the garden), and make sure the plant in question is positioned where he can't reach it, as even though it may be non-toxic, purchased plants could have been sprayed against disease or pests.

Think carefully about where you site plants anyway as wagging tails can send pots on low tables crashing to the floor, where broken crockery or glass may pose an additional hazard, or he may knock them off windowsills while checking to see who it is coming up the drive. A pot on the floor may be far more interesting than when it was on a higher surface and went largely ignored (or was considered off-limits), especially if the soil is spilling out. Some dogs may also view any exposed soil in plant pots as something fun to dig in, or possibly a place to toilet in, so don't leave him unsupervised with (safe) plants he can access until you are absolutely confident of his behaviour. And although you may have been careful to choose plants which aren't poisonous, remember that fertilizers and water-retaining granules that are not pet-friendly might have been added to the soil.

Cut plants also need to be carefully selected: plant food added to the water they stand in may be toxic, so make sure your dog can't knock over vases or reach them to drink out of. If buying a bouquet, pay attention to any greenery used to enhance the appearance of the flowers, too, as many of the popular choices are harmful.

PLANTS TO AVOID

Many favourite house plants can be harmful if nibbled at, and a few can be fatal. Plants you might prefer to avoid include those shown in the table on pages 97 and 98.

DOG-FRIENDLY HOUSE PLANTS

When checking whether plants are pet-friendly or best avoided, remember that common names can be misleading as they are sometimes used to describe more than one plant. While one may be safe, another may not be – for example, both the toxic *Dracaena* and the non-toxic *Chlorophytum comosum* go under the common name of Ribbon plant. Find out the scientific name, research it

Faking it: although it's possible to buy amazingly realistic artificial flowers and foliage plants, these aren't necessarily safer than the real thing; if your dog decides to chew them, the materials they're made from could prove dangerous to him.

(bearing in mind that absence from the many 'toxic' plant lists you can find on the internet does not mean it is safe), and if in doubt, don't buy it!

As far as I can determine, the plants in the table on page 99 are all said to be dog-friendly – although do check regularly on the internet as new research about the toxicity of various plants does pop up from time to time.

Windowsill nurseries

Windowsills can be ideal places for bringing on seeds and seedlings until they're ready to go outside into the garden, but don't forget that

❀ House plants to avoid ❀

Common name	Latin name	Comments
Aloe vera	*Aloe vera*	
Asparagus fern	*Asparagus densiflorus cv sprengeri*	Also known as Lace Fern
Azalea	*Rhododendron spp*	Can be fatal
Chrysanthemum	*Chrysanthemum spp*	
Cyclamen	*Cyclamen spp*	Also known as Persian violet: can be fatal
Dieffenbachia	*Dieffenbachia spp*	Also known as Dumb Cane: burning of the mouth and swelling of the tongue can obstruct breathing
Dracaena	*Dracaena spp*	Also known as Dragon tree, Ribbon plant
Elephant's ear	*Colocasia esculenta and Caladium hortulanum*	Also known as Caladium, Malanga
English ivy	*Hedera helix*	Also known as Common ivy, Sweetheart ivy, California ivy: can be fatal
Ficus	*Ficus benjamina*	Also known as Fig, Weeping Fig or India Rubber Plant
Fire lily	*Hippeastrum spp*	Also known as Amaryllis, Barbados Lily
Geranium	*Pelargonium spp*	
Hosta	*Hosta spp*	Also known as Plantain lily
Hydrangea	*Hydrangea spp*	
Kalanchoe	*Kalanchoe spp*	Also known as Chandelier plant, Mother of Millions
Mother-in-Law's Tongue	*Sansevieria trifasciata*	Also known as Good Luck Plant
Oleander	*Nerium oleander*	Also known as Rose Bay: can be fatal

Common name	Latin name	Comments
Peace Lily	*Spathiphylum spp*	
Philodendron	*Philodendron spp*	
Pothos	*Scindapsus spp and Epipremnum spp*	Also known as Devil's ivy, Silver vine
Sago Palm	*Cycas revoluta*	Also known as Cardboard Palm, Fern Palm: appears palatable to dogs and can be fatal
Schefflera	*Schefflera spp*	Also known as Umbrella plant, Octopus Tree
Swiss cheese plant	*Monstera deliciosa*	Also known as Ceriman, Mexican breadfruit
Yucca	*Yucca spp*	

they're also often at the perfect height for your dog to reach them.

CHRISTMAS

Even though you may not normally be a house plant sort of person, this situation tends to change around Christmas time. To your dog's amazement, things he normally associates with the outdoors suddenly begin to appear indoors, which may sometimes lead to a little confusion – such as a cocked leg against the tree you so considerately brought in for his use – and is certainly likely to intrigue him sufficiently to want to investigate more closely.

Christmas trees can cause all sorts of problems: shed needles can stick in the coat and feet, and some can be sharp enough to penetrate the skin, or the gut, if ingested. If branches are chewed, fir tree oils can irritate the mouth and stomach, plus any preservatives, pesticides, fertilizers and other chemicals used to enhance the appearance or prolong the tree's life may be toxic.

An artificial tree can look just as good, but may be subject to just as thorough and intense a

❀ Pet-friendly house plants ❀

Common name	Latin name	Comments
African violet	*Saintpaulia spp*	Also known as Cape marigold
Aluminium plant	*Pilea cadierei*	
American rubber plant	*Peperomia obtusifolia*	
Bamboo Palm	*Chamaedorea elegans*	Also known as Parlour Palm, Good Luck Palm
Boston fern	*Nephrolepis exaltata bostoniensis*	Also known as Sword Fern
Christmas cactus	*Schlumbergera bridgesii*	
Gerbera	*Gerbera jamesonii*	Also known as African Daisy
Living stones	*Lithops spp*	
Mosaic plant	*Fittonia argyroneura*	Also known as Nerve plant
Moth orchid	*Phalaenopsis spp*	
Prayer plant	*Calathea insignis*	
Prostrate Coleus	*Plectranthus oetendahlii*	
Roses	*Rosa spp*	Although the plants are non-toxic, thorns may cause injury – select thornless varieties if you are concerned
Spider plan	*Chlorophytum comosum*	Also known as Ribbon plant, Spider ivy
Swedish ivy	*Plectranthus australis*	Also known as Creeping Charlie
Sweetheart Hoya	*Hoya kerrii*	
Zebra Haworthia	*Haworthia fasciata*	
Zebra plant	*Calathea zebrina*	

Dog-friendly gardening

Christmas trees can be a source of amazement and fascination for many dogs, who will, naturally enough, want to inspect them more closely. (Courtesy Victoria Colville)

❀ Keep a close eye on puppies at all times

❀ Don't leave your dog alone in the room with the tree, whatever his age. Even older dogs can behave out of character on occasion

❀ Never hang food, and especially not chocolate novelties, from the branches as it's likely to be a temptation too far for even the best behaved of dogs. Human-grade chocolate – and especially dark chocolate – is highly toxic to dogs and can be fatal

❀ Cover any water container the tree is in so your dog isn't tempted to lap at it

Decorations

Christmas trees are not the only plants with the potential for being troublesome; if you're planning to deck the halls with holly and ivy, and steal a few kisses under the mistletoe, make sure you position them well out of reach of your dog, as they're all toxic. As mistletoe berries can be very poisonous, and holly berries slightly less so, it's a good idea to remove and safely dispose of them before arranging your decorations, as otherwise they may fall to the floor, unnoticed by everyone except your dog.

Gifts

Traditional plant gifts at Christmas include *Hippeastrums* (commonly called Amaryllis) and Hyacinths (*Hyacinthus orientalis*), either already growing or as bulbs in kits: both are toxic, although that other seasonal favourite, the Poinsettia (*Euphorbia pulcherrima*), is no longer thought to be highly poisonous. Nevertheless, it's still best to keep it away from pets if they are liable to try a nibble as it may cause nausea and vomiting at the very least.

CONSERVATORIES

Most of us are aware of the dangers of leaving dogs in cars on warm days, but conservatories can be just as fatal. Don't assume it's safe to leave

scrutiny, and if chewed on, can be just as much of a health risk.

Baubles, tinsel and other decorations may also be sampled with adverse effects, while chewing on the electrical cables of fairy lights can lead to electrical shocks and burns.

You don't have to ban Christmas trees from your house, though; most dogs soon grasp the idea that it's not a new toy for their amusement, and simply treat it as part of the furniture. But to be on the safe side and avoid the necessity of an emergency dash to the vet when you should all be settling down to Christmas dinner, it's wise to observe the following points:

him in there just because the sky is overcast – if it clears and the sun comes out, the temperature can quickly rise dangerously high for your pet, causing him to overheat. The same applies to greenhouses: if you need to restrict your dog's access to certain areas of the house, choose a room which will maintain a constant comfortable temperature.

Conservatories often have slippery floors, too; while this makes them easy to clean and perhaps accounts for their popularity as places to confine a dog, it's often not an ideal surface for him to walk on. Boisterous youngsters moving at speed may slide or be unable to stop and collide with something; older dogs may find it hard to to rise to their feet from a lying position and to maintain their balance while moving, while those of any age may suffer injury due to increased strain placed on joints and ligaments. It's an unforgiving surface to fall on, an uninviting one to lie on, and some dogs are afraid of moving across them. Putting down some rugs or matting needn't cost much, but will provide a safer surface with better grip which your dog will appreciate.

Visit Hubble and Hattie on the web: www.hubblrandhattie.com and www.hubbleandhattie • blogspot.com
 f **twitter** • *Details of all books • Special offers • Newsletter • New book news •*

Garden emergencies

Prevention is always better than cure, of course, but accidents can and do happen, despite an owner's best efforts to prevent them.

Although the information given in this chapter has been checked by a veterinary surgeon, it is not intended to be a substitute for first-hand veterinary advice and attention. As circumstances can vary, you should also regard the following suggestions about what to do in the event of various emergencies as guidelines, rather than hard-and-fast rules.

Do take some canine first aid training if the opportunity arises: courses are available, both online and at various colleges, or you might ask your vet to run one. At the very least, equip yourself with a good canine first aid book – and read it! – (see *Further reading*), and first aid kit, and always err on the side of caution and seek professional help if you have any concerns about your dog's health and wellbeing.

FIRST AID KIT

Either buy a ready-made first aid kit for your dog, or make up your own, but do keep everything together in one container or bag so it's easy to find, and whatever you need is ready to hand.

As a minimum include:

✿ Cotton wool
✿ Latex gloves
✿ Wound dressings
✿ Selection of bandages
✿ Adhesive tape
✿ Tweezers
✿ Tick-removing tool
✿ Blunt-nosed, curved scissors
✿ Alcohol-free wound-cleaning wipes
✿ Sachets of sterile saline solution

CUTS AND WOUNDS

Most minor cuts or grazes your dog sustains can usually be dealt with by gently bathing with a saline solution (1 teaspoon of table salt dissolved in 1 pint/500ml of warm water), and then leaving it uncovered. Keep an eye on it, and should the area become reddened, painful or oozy, or if you are in any way concerned about the injury, take your dog to the vet. Calendula tincture or cream can be a useful addition to your first aid kit for the treatment of cuts, as it can help reduce inflammation, prevent infection, and promote healing.

Veterinary attention will also be needed for cuts which have gone through the full thickness of the skin and need stitching. Cover with a dressing, if necessary, to keep it clean while on the way to the surgery, but don't apply any creams, lotions or powders. If there is heavy bleeding, cover with a sterile pad and bandage firmly over the top to keep the dressing in place while you take your dog to the vet. If blood seeps through, apply another pad and bandage and, if possible, raise the injured area as this will help lessen blood flow. Carry your dog to the car rather than asking him to walk, and keep an eye out for signs of shock developing (see also *page 110*).

BITES AND STINGS

We're lucky in the UK that there are very few dangerous venomous creatures, but the same isn't true elsewhere. Outside of the UK, check with your local veterinary practice which animals, reptiles and insects could pose a problem if your dog comes into contact with them, and what action you should take in the event of him getting bitten or stung.

Insect stings

Bee and wasp stings usually only cause a little

localized swelling and irritation. If the sting is still in place, carefully remove it with tweezers. In the case of bee stings, take care not to squeeze the attached venom sac as you do so. Use a cold compress to reduce pain and swelling; if you like, you could try the traditional remedy of applying vinegar to a wasp sting or a paste of bicarbonate of soda mixed with water to a bee sting, although your dog may lick it straight off. The homeopathic remedy *Apis mel* can also be helpful in such cases.

Stings can be more serious if around the mouth or throat, which could happen if your dog snaps at an insect as it buzzes past. If swelling interferes with his breathing, take him to the vet immediately. Anaphylactic shock – a life-threatening allergic reaction – can also sometimes occur, leading to difficulty in breathing, shock and collapse, in which case treat as for shock (page 110), and seek urgent veterinary attention.

Snake bites

Adders are the only venomous snakes in the UK, and unless you live close to heathland or south-facing downs, you're unlikely to find them in your garden – although you might see grass snakes or slow worms. Adders can be identified by a dark V or XS marking on their heads, and a zigzag pattern along their backs, whilst the inoffensive grass snake has a distinctive black and white or cream collar on the neck.

Slow worms (actually a type of legless lizard rather than a snake) are also harmless, and usually bronze, brown or grey in colour.

If you do think your dog has been bitten by an adder or other venomous snake, don't try and suck out the venom or wash it: carry him to the car and take him straight to the vet.

Cat bites and scatches

If your dog gets into a scrap with a feline trespasser, take him to the vet even if his injuries look fairly minor. Cat bites and scratches can be far nastier than they look: tips of claws can break off, and puncture wounds may be deeper than they look and more likely to become infected.

There may also be scratches to his eyes which will need to be checked using a special revealing dye.

BUZZ OFF

Wasps are generally useful around the garden, helping with pollination and killing aphids, and it's only once their job of bringing up the next generation is done that they're likely to become a nuisance.

At this point they become more dependent on sweet foodstuffs and will aggressively seek them out, which is not great news if you want to enjoy a cool drink in the garden. If you swat the wasp,

A Waspinator should help deter wasps from the garden. (Courtesy Waspinator Ltd)

you may not get rid of the problem, but actually increase it, as dying wasps can attract others.

Wasps usually only sting in self-defence but will defend their nests if disturbed: if you have one that you'd like removed don't try and do the job yourself but contact the local environmental health department.

If you prefer to adopt a greener approach, plan ahead by hanging up a Waspinator (see page 124 *Contacts and resources*) early in the year. Based on mediaeval technology, this fools foraging wasps into thinking that a nest is already present, and they'll steer clear for fear of being attacked. As a non-lethal solution it will help keep you and your pet safe whilst at the same time letting the wasps go about their lives rather than killing them.

HEATSTROKE

You may have heard warnings about not leaving your dog in the car on warm days because of the risk of heatstroke, but conservatories can be equally dangerous places to leave him as they can also become very hot.

This serious and potentially fatal condition can occur outdoors, too: help keep him from becoming overheated by exercising at the coolest times of day, and don't play energetic games in the garden either when it's hot. When he does join you in the garden, use paddling pools and frozen Kongs® to keep him entertained and cool, and encourage him to nap in a shady spot. If there isn't any suitable overhanging foliage in your garden, provide a parasol or mini-gazebo, or create some kind of garden feature which will offer protection from the sun. When the sun is at its highest and hottest – between 11am and 3pm – both of you will be better off indoors.

All dogs are susceptible to heatstroke, but those with dark coats or short noses, are very young or elderly, overweight, suffer from heart or respiratory disorders, or have had heatstroke in the past are especially high-risk. High humidity as well as high temperatures can also make it hard for your dog to lose heat, so keep a watchful eye on him and take action at the first sign of heatstroke.

The signs include:

- ❀ restlessness
- ❀ barking, whining
- ❀ excessive panting, drooling and shortness of breath. Do not wait until matters progress beyond this point, but seek veterinary help immediately

As the condition progresses, breathing becomes laboured and muscle tremors may occur; the gums appear dark red in colour and the eyes glassy and staring, followed in the final stages by seizures and unconsciousness.

If heatstroke is suspected, move your dog immediately to a shady area. If you have a paddling pool you can immerse him in that if the water is not too cold, but make sure you support his head above the surface. Otherwise, begin cooling him using cool – not cold or icy – water, concentrating on the inner upper thighs, armpits and base of the skull. Offer small sips of cool water every few minutes. Continue for ten minutes, and then take your dog to the vet even if he appears to have fully recovered.

DEHYDRATION

Dogs lose most of their excess body heat by panting. If your dog pants a lot – because he's been running around or playing, or because it's a hot day – he'll be losing a lot of moisture from his body as it evaporates into the air via his mouth and tongue. If he doesn't drink sufficiently to replace this lost fluid he is likely to become dehydrated, which can in turn lead to heatstroke, so ensure there's always a supply of clean, fresh water available outdoors as well as inside the house.

Older dogs may enjoy warming their bones in the garden with you on sunny days, but if joints are a bit stiff and creaky, may be reluctant to get up and take a drink as often as they should, so offer water regularly or leave a shallow bowl within easy reach. The first sign of dehydration is a dry mouth: the gums will feel tacky or dry when you touch them. Do not delay but seek veterinary advice.

Opposite: Particularly if he is having fun playing, your dog can easily overdo things and become overheated during warmer weather.

105

Swimming pools – even when covered – can be a potential hazard for your dog. (Courtesy Claire Colvin)

You can check for signs of dehydration by using a finger and thumb to gently pick up a fold of the loose skin at the base of your dog's neck where it meets the shoulders: when you release it, the skin should quickly flatten out again. If it remains 'tented,' your dog may be suffering from dehydration.

In older dogs a slow return to normal can also be due to a perfectly normal loss of skin elasticity, so check his gums, too. Gently press on the gum for one second and then release. The gum should go momentarily pale, with the colour returning quickly when the pressure is released: this is called the capillary refill time (CRT). If dehydrated, blood return occurs slowly, and the gum may also feel dry or tacky.

Other symptoms include loss of appetite, lethargy and sunken eyes. If you think your dog is dehydrated, take him to your vet.

HYPOTHERMIA

Temperatures don't need to be freezing for your dog to suffer from hypothermia – high wind chill factors can make it feel much colder than it really is. Most at risk are young puppies and elderly dogs, those which are underweight, who suffer from medical conditions such as diabetes or heart disease, small dogs, and dogs with thin coats and low levels of subcutaneous body fat.

It's unlikely to happen in your garden unless you accidentally shut him out there for any length of time but, nevertheless, if he falls into one of the 'at risk' categories, it is recommended that in cold weather you pop a jacket on him before he goes out to spend a penny, have a mooch around, or if you are out doing some training or playing with him. The sweater-style coats available will help keep more sparsely-haired tummies warm, particularly if your dog has short legs and is close to snow-covered ground.

DROWNING

Any water features in your garden should either be safe for dogs or securely fenced off. Unfortunately, even then, accidents can still happen: a gate carelessly left open, or a moment's lack of attention when visiting a friend's garden can lead to a curious or water-loving dog getting into difficulties.

Should this happen and your dog is unconscious, pick him up and hold him upside down by the back legs for 10-20 seconds so that water will drain out of his lungs and airways. If he's too big to do this, lie him on his side with his head lower than the rest of his body.

Check in his mouth and remove any obstructions, check for breathing and a pulse, and give artificial respiration or heart massage as necessary (see *Resuscitation* on page 109). Seek veterinary attention even if he recovers.

ELECTRIC SHOCK/ELECTROCUTION

The commonest cause of this is from your dog chewing through the cables of electrical appliances – flexes attached to mowers, leaf blowers, strimmers, hedge trimmers and other garden gadgets can wiggle temptingly, inviting a game of chase, pounce and bite. Keep him safely indoors while you are busy, and for your own safety (and just in case anyone unintentionally lets him out before you've finished and put everything away), always use a circuit breaker, too.

Electrical cables for lights or water pumps can be another source of danger, so either ensure they cannot be accessed, or use a safer power source, such as solar panels.

In the event of electrocution it's essential to switch off the electricity at the mains before touching your dog or the current could pass through you, too. Check for breathing and heartbeat and give artificial respiration or CPR as required (see overleaf). Treat any burns by cooling with water (see *Burns*, below,) and even if your dog appears to have had a lucky escape or be fully recovered, take him to the vet to be checked over.

BURNS

Burns can be caused by all sorts of things: dry heat from lawnmower engines, garden bonfires and barbeques (remember that sparks may fly through the air and land on your dog, even if he's at what

Encourage your dog to seek a shady area to nap in during warm weather, and take him indoors out of the sun when it's at its hottest. (Courtesy Val Borland)

you consider to be a safe distance); chemicals such as weedkiller, battery acid, creosote and other items lurking in the garden shed, and even scalds from hot liquids, such as that mug of tea you took out into the garden to drink. If you do accidentally tip a hot drink on a hairy dog, it's easy to miss signs of skin damage, so even though he may look fine, it's still best to take him to the vet for a check-up.

While causes may differ, treatment is essentially the same for all, involving cooling using water. If the coat has caught fire, smother any flames with a jacket, blanket or whatever else is available, or if hot, oily liquids are involved, blot up as much as possible using kitchen towel, paper tissues or toilet paper first. Use a continuous stream of water from a hosepipe, or soak towels and cool for a minimum of 10 minutes to stop burning and help reduce pain, then cover with a non-stick sterile dressing to keep the area clean and take your dog to the vet.

In the case of chemical burns, wear rubber gloves while treating your dog, and use plenty of water, taking care not to spread it across the rest of him, and continuing for at least 20 minutes. If his mouth is burned due to chewing at a container or licking at a spilt residue, flush out his mouth from back to front so it doesn't run down his throat. Take the container with you when you go to the vet.

One other form of burn which can affect your dog, especially if he has a pink nose or sparsely-coated areas is sunburn (see below).

SUNBURN

Sunbathing is a favourite summer activity in the garden for lots of dogs, but they don't always know when they've had enough. Those with thin coats, or areas where bare skin is exposed can be particularly susceptible to sunburn, so if you have a canine sun-worshipper, follow the same rules with your dog as for people: slip, slop and slap. Slip a thin cotton doggy T-shirt on him to help protect sparsely-covered chests and tums, and slop a sunblock on. Buy either a veterinary sunblock or use a high factor, unscented human one designed for sensitive skin (such as those for toddlers), but always try a small test patch first before applying more liberally. Although you can't slap a hat on your dog, you can encourage him to lie in the shade – maybe provided by an overhanging leafy tree – or you could put up a parasol.

It's probably best to keep him out of the sun during the summer between 11am and 3pm when the sun is at its highest and hottest. If your dog does become sunburnt, consult your vet as it can be painful and may be liable to become infected.

POISONING

Dogs do not instinctively know if something is bad for them, and this, coupled with insatiable curiosity and sometimes greed, can lead to accidental poisoning.

Not just plants but many garden products can be toxic, too, and some don't even need to be directly ingested to be harmful: chemicals coming into contact with the skin may be corrosive, or if paws are licked after treading on residues, this may be enough to cause your dog to become seriously ill.

Store all herbicides, pesticides, fertilizers, cleaning products and other chemicals out of reach of your dog: a product's claims to be organic or pet- and wildlife-friendly is no guarantee of its safety. Always read the instructions for use and all small print very thoroughly, and consider any potential risk to your dog carefully when deciding whether or not to use it.

Taking the view that anything liable to be toxic to people is likely to be harmful to your pet is a sensible one – but don't forget that there are also many things which are fine for us, but not dogs, such as grapes and onions. Chocolate is another item which can be fatal; and while it looks good on flowerbeds, using a cocoa mulch by-product can prove equally terminal if ingested by your dog.

Symptoms of poisoning can vary considerably but may include:

* lack of co-ordination
* shivering, tremors
* drooling, panting
* vomiting, diarrhoea
* convulsions
* loss of consciousness

If you see your dog eating something poisonous, or suspect that he may have done, take him to the vet as quickly as possible to have an injection that will make him vomit. Traditional emetics (to induce vomiting) can be very caustic when given orally, or can cause more harm than the poison itself. In addition, you may be wasting valuable time trying to encourage your dog to vomit which could be better spent getting him to the vet quickly. Give your vet as much information as you can about the substance swallowed, how much, and how long ago, and take along to the surgery any containers or samples of plants to ensure correct identification and treatment.

If the poison is on his skin, use clean, lukewarm water (and, if necessary, a mild shampoo as not all poisons are water-soluble) to wash it off. Prevent him from licking the area by using a cone collar or muzzle, or by covering the area with a T-short, then take him straight to the vet.

RESUSCITATION
Heavy bleeding, electrocution, drowning and shock may all cause your dog's breathing and/or heart to

stop. This is an emergency situation and you should seek urgent veterinary attention, but while waiting for professional assistance you can also take action yourself. Even though you may not be successful in reviving your dog, you will have at least given him a chance.

First of all, make sure that the area is safe, after which place your dog lying down on his right-hand side. Open his mouth to check that nothing is blocking the airway, removing anything that is. Stretch out his head and neck to straighten the airway and listen carefully for the sound of breathing – it may be very shallow and faint. Look along the line of his ribcage for any movement; if unsure, try holding a piece of dry grass or strand of hair by the nostrils to see if it moves. Be very careful of your own safety, as your face will be in a vulnerable position should your dog suddenly recover consciousness.

If you think your dog may have eaten something poisonous contact your vet immediately; take a sample of what you think he has eaten with you when you go to the surgery.

109

If your dog isn't breathing, rub his sides briskly for 30 seconds: if there's no response, draw his tongue slightly forward and place your hands round the muzzle to keep the jaws closed. Put your mouth over the nostrils to form a seal and blow just hard enough to make the chest rise. Remove your mouth and allow the lungs to empty, then replace it and blow again, giving one breath of air every 3-5 seconds.

Check after every 4 or 5 breaths that there's still a heartbeat by either placing your hand on the ribcage to feel for a heartbeat, or feeling for a pulse on the inside of a hindleg where it meets the body. If the heart has stopped, put the fleshy part of the heel of one hand on the ribcage just behind your dog's elbow, place your other hand on top and quickly and firmly press downward and forward toward the neck. Repeat 60-100 times a minute. If you're dealing with a small dog, grasp the chest just behind the elbows with one hand instead, and, supporting the back with your other hand, squeeze quickly and firmly to compress the ribcage.

After every 5 compressions give a breath of air (after every 3 compressions if a small dog), and stop if the heart starts beating again. Only ever give artificial respiration if there is no breathing, and only ever give heart massage if the heart has stopped.

SHOCK

Heavy bleeding, dehydration and heart failure are just a few of the causes of shock; this is a medical emergency which can be fatal, so needs urgent attention. Signs that shock is developing include rapid breathing and pulse rate, colour is slow to return to the gums when pressure is applied with the tip of a finger (see *Dehydration*), paws and ears feel cool or cold, and the dog appears weak and lethargic.

As shock develops, breathing becomes shallow and the pulse irregular, the gums become pale or blue, and the dog finally lapses into unconsciousness.

Keep him warm (even if it is summer), quiet and still, and if he's unconscious raise the hindquarters so they are slightly higher than the head. Stem any obvious bleeding (see *Cuts and wounds*), keep an eye on breathing and pulse, and get him to a vet as quickly as possible.

TTOUCH EAR WORK

If you only ever learn one of the special Tellington-Touch 'TTouches' (see *Enjoying the garden*) then make it Ear Work, which can help calm, or even be a lifesaver in an emergency.

"When our Maremma Orsa bloated she went into shock – rapid breathing, white gums and collapse," recalls Janet Finlay. "During the half hour drive to the vet, I did continuous Ear Work, and by the time we arrived, Orsa was able to walk into the vet's and had some colour returning to her gums. She had surgery and is still going strong – but I firmly believe that the Ear Work also played a vital part in saving her life: I doubt she would have survived the journey without it."

Ear Work also helped Harvey when he somehow managed to lacerate a major blood vessel in his tongue while out in the garden: "The amount of blood he was losing was scary," says Deborah Kieboom. "Naturally, it had to happen out of hours, and the nearest 24-hour vet was a 25-minute drive away; Harvey was getting very agitated and every time he moved his mouth in any way blood just poured out. I was scared stiff he wouldn't make it, but was very grateful I knew about Ear Work – I did long, slow slides down his ears the whole way, and finally we reached the vet's. Their faces paled when they saw the amount of blood covering us both – they thought I'd been exaggerating when I rang. Harvey was rushed into emergency surgery so fast they even forgot to ask me to sign the consent form!

"Afterwards they commented that they were amazed at what good condition Harvey was in considering the amount of blood he'd lost – I put it down to the Ear Work."

HOW TO DO IT

Ear Work is easy to learn, most dogs enjoy it and it can be very comforting. Position yourself so you

Tellington-Touch Ear Work can be a lifesaver in an emergency. (Courtesy Sarah Fisher)

and your dog are facing in the same direction and use the back of one hand to stroke softly along the outside edge of one ear, while gently supporting his head with your other hand.

Next, take the ear between thumb and forefinger and slide them along the length, from the base right out to the end. At the tip is an acupressure 'shock' point: make a small circle there with the tip of your forefinger to stimulate it, and then slide your fingers off.

Hold the ear so your thumb is on the outer, furry side, and move your hand slightly with each stroke so that you cover every part of the ear. If your dog has upright ears slide your fingers in an upward direction: if they flop downward, slide your fingers outward in a horizontal direction.

Be gentle and vary your speed according to the effect you want: working slowly will help calm and relax, while going faster will invigorate. If you'd like to see a psctical demonstration of this and other Tellington-TTouches, visit the website at www.tilleyfarm.org.uk.

Goodbye, dear friend

The death of a much-loved dog can't always be predicted, but when illness or old age start to become too much of a burden for your faithful friend, you can at least ensure he has a painless and dignified end: letting him go gently and with love may be one of the hardest things you ever have to do, but is your last great gift to him.

Once his spirit has passed on, you will need to decide what to do with his physical remains. It's important to give this some thought before it becomes a reality, as closer to the time you may find yourself too distressed to cope with making decisions and arrangements – or could end up being pressured by others into making a choice you will later regret.

As any owner will know, there is no such thing as 'just a dog,' and the loss of a much-loved, four-legged friend can be as painful and distressing as that of any human friend or relative. For some, laying his body to rest in a way you feel appropriate acknowledges the importance of the part he played in your life, and the love you shared. Being able to visit a grave or create some kind of a memorial can also be therapeutic and help as you journey through the grieving process. Just as your garden played a part in your pet's life, so it can in his passing.

TRADITION

Burying a beloved dog with reverence and care is a long-standing tradition that stretches back at least 14,000 years. Canine burial sites have been found all over the world, the dogs sometimes sharing a grave with their owner, and often with special grave goods included such as bowls or a juicy beef bone.

In more recent years official pet cemeteries have sprung up, a phenomenon which began in 1896 when New York veterinary surgeon

Dr Samuel Johnson allowed a bereaved friend to bury his dog in his apple orchard. Others heard of the kindness and asked if they could do so also, and over 70,000 pets have since been buried at what is now known as Hartsdale Pet Cemetery.

In 1899 Le Cimetiere des Chiens at Asnieres on the outskirts of Paris became the first European pet cemetery, while in 1979 the Rosa Bonheur Memorial Park in Maryland, USA made news headlines when it became the first cemetery in the world to allow humans to be buried alongside their pets. Our ancestors of 14,000 years ago would have wondered at the fuss made over a practice they considered perfectly normal.

BURIAL OR CREMATION?

Space, finances and religious beliefs, as well as personal feelings, will all play a part in your decision of what to do with your dog's physical remains when he passes on. You can allow your vet to take care of this for you, or you can be more personally involved: although taxidermy, cryomation (freeze-drying), or resomation (a water/alkali-based process) are alternative options, the most popular choices for owners are still either burial or cremation.

Burial

Current UK legislation allows you to bury your pet in the garden of the house where he lived. If you have more than one property, then technically it should be at the address he was resident at when he died, although this is something of a grey area and probably unlikely to be enforced. You cannot bury him in a friend's garden, however, or at all if his remains are considered for some reason to be a hazard to human health, which is something your vet will determine. Elsewhere, check on the

legalities as these vary from one country to another. There may also be regulations regarding depth and location of burial, and about marking the spot: check with your local authority if you aren't sure.

If you want to bury your dog at home, consider where you'd like this to be: maybe a particular favourite spot where he liked to spend time, near where you sit and relax, or which you can see from a window of your house. It should, however, be somewhere you won't be disturbing in the future with deep digging, and should also be away from water courses.

Depending on soil type, a home burial can involve hard digging. Environment Agency rules for licensed pet cemeteries stipulate a minimum 0.5m of soil between pet and ground surface – just over one and a half feet – but go deeper than this if you can, allowing at least 2ft (0.60m) in heavy soils, and 3ft (0.91m) in light ones. Kevin Spurgeon of Dignity Pet Crematorium advises: "The deeper the better, as it will minimise the risk of remains being disturbed at some future date by anyone cultivating a border or planting a tree or shrub. You can also protect the site by placing slabs either below or above ground level to prevent disturbance of the grave by a gardener, wildlife, or other dogs you own."

You can buy a special coffin to place your pet in if you wish – you'll find plenty of suppliers online offering a choice of materials, including eco-friendly options such as cardboard, willow, bamboo and jute. Alternatively, you can simply wrap him in a cotton sheet – but avoid plastic bags or materials that take a long time to degrade or which are non-porous. "It's essential to choose materials that will break down, allowing nature to take its course," says Kevin, "Otherwise the area is liable to end up becoming waterlogged, which can be really distressing."

Planning for the future

Burying your pet's remains or interring his ashes in your garden may seem the perfect final gesture, but can have consequences in the future if you decide to move, so think very carefully before taking

this course of action. When selling a house, new owners may not be enthusiastic about the prospect of animal remains in the garden, especially if more than one has been laid to rest there. It's only fair to warn them, however, in case they plan any major changes, and will give you peace of mind that your pet's remains won't be disturbed.

A house move also means you won't be able to visit his last resting place – unless the new owners are exceptionally understanding, and even then their patience may wear thin if you want to make frequent trips.

Exhuming him so you can take him with you may not be possible if he was cremated, or if plants have spread their roots and grown out over the top of his resting place: and depending on soil type and the amount of time which has passed, there may not be much by way of physical remains anyway. It can also be a distressing process which needs organising well in advance as I can personally testify after conducting a frantic, muddy and tearful search in the pouring rain for our much-loved lurcher while the removal men waited outside.

Not in my back garden

Not everyone feels comfortable with the thought of burying a pet – however beloved – in the garden. There may also be practical reasons why it isn't possible, such as the size of your pet, because you rent rather than own your property, live in an area where pet burial isn't permitted, or because, at some point in the future, a house move is likely. In such instances, the alternatives are cremation (see overleaf), or using a pet cemetery.

There are pet cemeteries scattered around the country, but as they all vary, make sure you visit in advance to ensure it fits all your personal preferences. Some resemble human cemeteries with neatly tended formal plots and headstones, whilst others offer 'green' burials in more rustic surroundings, often with a tree planted on top of the site. If you wish, there are even a few pet cemeteries where you can reserve a plot for yourself, too.

During your visit ask whether you will be given

(Courtesy Dignity Pet Crematorium)

a contract that will cover protection of the grave site for a set period, as well as about maintenance fees, visiting times, and whether you will be allowed to erect a memorial – and what restrictions there might be, if so. As pet cemeteries sometimes go out of business, you should also ask what would happen to your pet's grave if this happened.

Cremation

Cremation is usually the most popular choice amongst owners, and is generally cheaper than burial in a pet cemetery. Most vets have contracts with pet crematoria which collect pets for individual or mass cremation on a weekly basis. Like cemeteries, pet crematoria can vary greatly in the services they offer, and it is best to do your own research on local alternatives before choosing the company that your vet offers you, as their decision may be based on convenience or cost rather than the best service for your dog.

If you choose individual cremation you have various options regarding what to do with his ashes: some pet crematoria have special gardens of remembrance where they can be scattered, or you may prefer to do this at a place or along a walk you used to take together which holds special memories for you.

You can inter them in the garden if you prefer, or keep them in an urn – some owners wish to have their own ashes mixed and scattered with those of their pet when they die themselves. It is currently illegal for a pet's ashes to be re-cremated alongside his owner at a human crematorium, or buried with you in a human cemetery unless the site has a separate permit to also bury pets.

Cremation also gives you another option: that of placing your pet's ashes in a large planter, which you can then grow a plant in, or maybe seasonal bulbs that will flower in succession throughout the year. This creates an attractive memorial which can raise a smile as you see it growing and remember your dog, and if you move you will still be able to take his last resting place with you. If you prefer, artificial silk plants can look wonderfully realistic, will involve no maintenance beyond replacement

in due course, and ensure a colourful, year-round display.

CREATING A MEMORIAL

Be guided by your own personal feelings regarding how – or even whether – you create some kind of special memorial to a beloved dog, but don't let what other people think put you off. Memorials are a time-honoured custom for pets and nothing to be embarrassed about: most owners will understand the underlying sentiment in the ancient Greek epitaph which reads:

"You who pass by, if you do mark this monument, do not laugh, I beg you, though it is a dog's grave. Tears fell for me, and the earth was heaped above me by a master's hand, who likewise engraved these words on my tomb."

Whether your dog's remains lie in your garden or elsewhere, making a part of your garden a special place in memory of him can be a wonderful way of paying tribute.

Memorial stones

Many companies make a range of pet memorial headstones and plaques that can be inscribed according to your wishes. If you prefer, you can make your own, which can feel more personal as well as giving you something practical to do. A large, smooth cobble with a name painted on it is simple but effective; or if you want something larger, buy a paving slab from a DIY centre or builder's merchant that you can decorate. These can be bought singly, come in a variety of sizes, colours and materials, and offer scope for being placed horizontally, vertically, or sloping at an angle to the ground.

You can also buy preformed stepping stone slabs in the shape of flower heads that can look very decorative. If you enjoy craft projects, you might even think of producing something more ambitious, using stained glass or mosaic rather than paint.

If a headstone or plaque isn't your style, a piece of statuary can be an attractive way of commemorating your dog: you can often find a good selection at larger garden centres. If you like the idea of something functional, then consider a seat or bench to sit on, or maybe a birdbath.

Lighting

The Candle Ceremony is a lovely idea which began when a small group of people on an internet chat room were discussing the ways they remembered pets who had died. When Lisa Sayer mentioned that every Monday evening she lit a candle, several others said they'd like to do it, too, and so a time was set and a format produced for a brief commemorative ceremony, and the first 'Bridge list' (after the Rainbow Bridge poem) was posted online on March 15, 1993.

Within two weeks the Candle Ceremony had gone global, and today owners all over the world continue to join in. If you'd like to participate, you can find details at www.petloss.com. When the weather is good, it can be nice to light your candle outside in the garden, maybe by the place where your dog is buried. You can buy pretty little lanterns which can be used safely outdoors with a tealight inside, and which will prevent the flame being blown out by the breeze. Solar garden lights can also be used to mark the spot.

Trees

A tree can be a striking memorial to a dog, and one which will last for generations; in the case of a male dog, you may also feel it to be particularly appropriate! Some trees also have symbolic associations in mythology and folklore: Oak represents strength, Apple magic and happiness, Rowan good luck and protection, while in Japan, Cherry blossom represents mortality and the transient nature of life. Make sure you choose sensibly, though, and pick a tree which is not going to grow so tall that it will eventually need to be chopped down. Choose a location where it won't block views, the branches interfere with overhead cables, or the roots cause damage to paths, walls, foundations or drains.

If you don't have room for the tree of your

(*Courtesy Kevin Spurgeon*)

The Monday evening Candle Ceremony is a lovely way of remembering a faithful friend.

117

CAESAR

1985 - 1995

A loving friend to all

XXX

(Courtesy Dignity Pet Crematorium)

locations – which might offer an acceptable alternative.

PLANTING SUGGESTION

If space is limited, you can buy apple trees grafted onto different rootstocks which limit their size – some can even be successfully grown in containers. Many other species of tree have dwarf varieties, or you could grow one as a bonsai specimen, which have additional symbolic associations with harmony, peace and balance.

Plants

Whether your pet's remains lie in your garden or elsewhere, plants can make a beautiful living tribute, and a way of creating a special place where you can remember him.

If you don't use evergreen plants, think of ways you can keep your chosen spot – be it a whole bed or a single container – looking special during the winter months when blooms and foliage die back. Look for plants that have sculptural qualities when leaves have fallen, or maybe place a piece of statuary there so it doesn't look bare and forlorn at this time.

Otherwise, the usual gardening constraints apply: pick plants that will be happy with the soil, sun and other growing conditions, and if you have (or are planning to acquire) another dog be careful about toxicity if he will have access to that area. One other piece of sage advice is offered by Kevin Spurgeon: "Choose healthy plants you are pretty sure will survive, because if they don't, it can result in sad rather than happy memories."

CHOOSING MEMORIAL PLANTS

Obviously it's important that the plants you choose for your pet's memorial are ones which will give you pleasure to look at, but searching out those which have a similar name to that of your dog, or particular associations can be fun and give your special area a personal touch.

A rose by any other name

As many plants either share or have more than one

choice, there are plenty of tree planting schemes – within cities and urban areas as well as in rural common name which can vary between regions as well as countries, they also have a unique scientific botanical name in order to avoid any confusion. Written in italics, these are usually Latin-based and are recognised worldwide, whatever the local language.

The system of classifying and naming plants used today was originally devised by Swedish botanist Carolus Linnaeus during the 18th century. The first name (genus) is the equivalent of your surname, linking all plants in the same family; the second name (species) is like your Christian name, distinguishing between individuals within that family. In the case of cultivars – plants deliberately created or which have appeared by chance – there may be a third name, not italicised and placed within single quotation marks.

Cultivars are often named after people, or chosen to attract buyers, and when Linnaeus first set about his enormous task of classification, he named many after friends, colleagues and other botanists such as Forsythia for William Forsyth and Banksia after Sir Joseph Banks.

You can do something similar when trying to find an appropriate plant to commemorate your pet, by choosing one which either carries the same name or echoes a sentiment you feel, such as 'Sweet Memories' or 'Sweet Dreams.' If this idea appeals to you, it's worth visiting the RHS website at www.rhs.org.uk which has a useful plant finder section; as well as checking out names it will help you locate sellers, too. Some companies even offer a 'Name a rose' service if you want an especially unique memorial plant.

Say it with flowers

In Victorian times, the 'language of flowers' was a popular way for lovers to secretly communicate, by exchanging different plants which had various meanings associated with them. This floral code in fact stretches even further back to mediaeval times, and is a tradition you might like to continue by growing plants that have a particular meaning you associate with your dog.

Some ideas include:

- Blue violet – faithfulness
- Calendula – affection, joy, remembrance
- Campanula – I think of you
- Carnation – devoted love
- Forget me not – faithful love
- Lambs Ears – gentleness
- Pansy – loving thoughts
- Poppy – rest, eternal sleep
- Rose – love
- Salvia (blue) – I think of you
- Stonecrop – tranquillity
- Sunflower (dwarf) – adoration
- Sweet pea – goodbye, departure, thank you for a lovely time
- Sweet William – gallantry, perfection
- Violet – faithfulness, devotion
- Zinnia – lasting affection, thoughts of absent friends

Some flowers can have a more specific as well as a generalised meaning, depending on colour. Roses, for example, are associated with love, but a red one symbolises eternal love, yellow joy, friendship and freedom, white innocence and purity, and a pink rose grace and beauty. Similarly, a red carnation says 'My heart aches for you,' and a pink one 'I will never forget you.'

PLANTING SUGGESTION

The feathery blue-green foliage and vibrant colours of the California Poppy (*Eschscholzia californica*) produce a wonderfully cheering display which can really raise the spirits. Drought-tolerant and easy to grow, they prefer full sun and poor, well drained soil, and as they will self-seed year after year, a packet of seeds can be good value, too. Although not on the ASPCA's extensive list of toxic plants (see *Plants for the garden*), they may have toxic properties if ingested.

Herbs

A herb garden – which could be a whole bed, a trough, planter or single pot (see *Plants for the garden*) – is another option you might like to consider. As well as being a practical, aromatic and

119

Californian poppies.

attractive addition to the garden, herbs have as long a tradition of associated meanings as flowers, including:

✿ Chamomile – wisdom
✿ Garlic – courage, protection against evil
✿ Lavender – love, devotion
✿ Marigold – affection, sorrow
✿ Marjoram – joy, happiness
✿ Mint – wisdom, virtue
✿ Parsley – merriment, energy, lasting pleasure
✿ Rosemary – remembrance, loyalty, love, immortality
✿ Sage – wisdom, respect
✿ Spearmint – warm sentiment
✿ Thyme – daring, bravery, courage, vigour, strength

THE PERFECT MEMORIAL

Sometimes the perfect plant memorial is right in front of you, as Val Borland discovered: "When we moved to our current house, some friends bought us a lovely crab apple tree as a house-warming present, which looked beautiful in the middle of the lawn in the back garden.

"It was a bigger house than our last one, so we were also able to finally realise my husband's dream of a German Shepherd puppy to join our two Springer Spaniels. Breeya duly arrived and had a great time cavorting around the garden with the others; all was fine until the day we went to the back door to find a short twig where there had once been a beautiful healthy tree. She'd chomped right through the middle of our house-warming present, and the remains were scattered all about the garden.

"When she died we talked about planting a tree in memory of her – and then we realised we already had her special tree ... the stumpy crab apple which is now a glorious mass of pink flowers every spring."

MOVING ON

Organizing a small ceremony, arranging for some kind of memorial such as a plaque, planting a tree, or creating a special memorial area in your garden can bring comfort as well as giving you something practical to do as you move through the grieving process. Sometimes it only slightly diminishes

Floyd relaxes under Breeya's special tree. (Courtesy Val Borland)

121

Dog-friendly gardening

A bench in a favourite walking area can be a great memorial, and the perfect place to hold a small ceremony with friends, both four- and two-legged.

the awful sense of loss, however, and once such tasks are completed, you're left with little else to do except nurse your heartache. Bereavement touches everyone differently, and each loss is a new experience. Deep feelings of grief can persist not just for days, but continue for weeks, months or even years, and can affect you physically as well as emotionally.

Although it's now recognised that the intensity of grief felt is comparable to, and often stronger than that felt following a human bereavement, not everyone will understand this, or why you seem to be unable to move on. Being able to talk to a sympathetic listener can be helpful, but because the loss of an animal often involves such very deep, personal and private thoughts and feelings, it's sometimes hard to share them, even with close friends or relatives. Or maybe you've tried, but there's been a lack of understanding of just how much your four-legged friend meant to you. A trained bereavement counsellor may be easier to talk to (see *Useful contacts and resources*), or if you are really feeling overwhelmed by your feelings and are struggling to cope, do see your GP.

THE BEST PLACE TO BURY A DOG

Whatever the decision you make about the last resting place for your dog, keep in mind the wonderfully compassionate and wise words written by Ben Hur Lampman in response to a query he received while working as a columnist on *The Oregonian* in 1926:

"There are various places in which a dog may be buried. We are thinking now of a setter, whose coat was flame in the sunshine and who, so far as we are aware, never entertained a mean or unworthy thought.

This setter is buried beneath a cherry tree, under four feet of garden loam, and at its proper season the cherry tree strews petals on the green lawn of his grave. Beneath a cherry tree, or an apple, or any flowering shrub of the garden, is an excellent place to bury a dog. Beneath such trees, such shrubs, he slept in the drowsy summer, or gnawed at a flavoured bone, or lifted his head to challenge some strange intruder.

These are good places, in life or in death. Yet it is a small matter, and it touches sentiment more than anything else. For if the dog be well remembered, if sometimes he leaps through your dreams actual as in life, eyes kindling, questing, asking, laughing, begging, it matters not at all where that dog sleeps at long and at last. On a hill where the wind is unrebuked, and the trees are roaring, or beside a stream he knew in puppyhood, or somewhere in the flatness of a pasture land, where most exhilarating cattle graze. It is all one to the dog, and all one to you, and nothing is gained, and nothing is lost – if memory lives.

But there is one best place to bury a dog. One place that is best of all. If you bury him in this spot, the secret of which you must already have, he will come to you when you call – come to you over the grim, dim frontier of death, and down the well-remembered path, and to your side again. And though you call a dozen living dogs to heel, they shall not growl at him, nor resent his coming, for he belongs there. People may scoff at you, who see no lightest blade of grass bent by his footfall, who hear no whimper, people who may never really have had a dog. Smile at them, for you shall know something that is hidden from them, and which is well worth the knowing.

The one best place to bury a good dog is in the heart of his master."

Ben Hur Lampman 1896-1954

Contacts & resources

✿ ACTIVITIES
Agility
Agility Bits
www.agilitybits.co.uk

Agilitynet
www.agilitynet.com

American Kennel Club
www.akc.org

The Kennel Club
www.thekennelclub.org.uk

Treibball
www.americantreibballassociation.org

✿ ADVICE, RESCUE AND WELFARE
Dogs Trust
www.dogstrust.org.uk

Battersea Dogs & Cats Home
www.battersea.org.uk

Dog Theft Action
www.dogtheftaction.com

✿ DOG ID
National Dog Tattoo Register
www.dog-register.co.uk

Petlog
Tel: 0844 4633 999
www.petlog.org.uk

✿ GARDENING
Green roofs
www.livingroofs.org

www.thegreenroofcentre.co.uk

Poisonous plants
Lists of toxic and pet-friendly plants
www.aspca.org
www.dogstrust.org.uk

Royal Horticultural Society
www.rhs.org.uk

✿ HEALTH AND HYGIENE
Dogs Doorbell
Tel: 01263 860393
www.dogsdoorbell.co.uk

Kennels and runs
www.kennelstore.co.uk

Pee Post
www.canineconcepts.co.uk

Pet Loo
Armitages Clean Green Dog Loo is widely available
at garden centres, pet shops and online but in
the event of difficulty locating a supplier contact
Armitages on its website email form.
www.armitages.co.uk

Rodent control
www.ufaw.org.uk/rodents

Safe4 Disinfectant and Odour Killer
www.safe4disinfectant.com

Ticks: Boreliosis and Associated Diseases
Awareness UK (BADA-UK)
www.bada-uk.org

Waspinator
www.waspinator.co.uk

Wormeries
www.originalorganics.co.uk

❀ PET LOSS
Association of Pet Cemeteries and Crematoria
www.appcc.org.uk

Blue Cross Pet Bereavement Support Service
Tel: 0800 096 6606
Email: pbssmail@bluecross.org.uk
www.bluecross.org.uk

Dignity Pet Crematorium
Brickfields
Odiham Road
Winchfield
Hook
Hants RG27 8BU
Tel: 01252 844572
www.dignitypetcrem.co.uk

Pet loss grief/memorial sites
Lost and Fond
www.lostandfond.co.uk

World-wide Monday Candle Ceremony
www.petloss.com

Pet loss support programme
www.ease-animals.org.uk

❀ TELLINGTON-TOUCH
TTouch UK
Tilley Farm
Bath
BA2 0AB
Tel: 01761 471182
www.tilleyfarm.org.uk

TTouch Canada
5435 Rochdell Road
Vernon BC1VB 3E8

Canada
www.ttouch.ca

TTouch USA
PO Box 3793
Santa Fe
New Mexico 87501
USA
www.ttouch.com

TTouch South Africa
www.ttouchsa.co.za

TOYS
Boomer ball
www.boomerball.com

Bubble machines
www.dog-bubble-machines.co.uk

Company of Animals
Range of interactive and treat-dispensing toys
Tel: 01932 566696
www.companyofanimals.co.uk

Kong®
www.kongcompany.com

Nina Ottoson Interactive Toys
www.nina-ottoson.com

❀ TRAINING
Association of Pet Dog Trainers UK
PO Box 17
Kempsford
GL7 4WZ
England
Tel: 01285 810811
www.apdt.co.uk

Association of Pet Dog Trainers (US)
www.apdt.com

Clicker training
www.clickertraining.com

Dog-friendly gardening

Really Reliable Recall
By Leslie Nelson, Healthy Dog Productions (DVD)

WILDLIFE

British Hedgehog Preservation Society
www.britishhedgehogs.org.uk

Buglife
www.buglife.org.uk

The Bumblebee Conservation Trust
www.bumblebeeconservation.org.uk

Froglife
www.froglife.org

Royal Society for Protection of Birds
www.rspb.org.uk

St Tiggywinkles
www.sttiggywinkles.org.uk

FURTHER READING

Getting in Touch with your Dog by Linda Tellington-Jones (Kenilworth Press)

100 Ways to Train the Perfect Dog by Sarah Fisher and Marie Miller (David & Charles)

Dog Games: stimulating play to entertain your dog and you by Christiane Blenski (Hattie & Hubble)

Emergency First Aid for Dogs – Home and Away by Martin Bucksch (Hubble and Hattie)

Goodbye, Dear Friend by Virginia Ironside (JR Books)

My dog is blind ... but lives life to the full! by Nicole Horsky (Hubble and Hattie)

My dog is deaf ... but lives life to the full! by Jennifer Willms (Hubble and Hattie)

My dog has arthritis ... but lives life to the full! by Gill Carrick (Hubble and Hattie)

Losing a Pet by Jane Matthews (Smallbooks)

Your Dog magazine (Bourne Publishing) www.yourdog.co.uk

Living with an Older Dog by David Alderton and Derek Hall (Hubble & Hattie)

DOG-FRIENDLY GARDENS TO VISIT

Attadale Gardens, Wester Ross: www.attadalegardens.com
Cae Hir Gardens, Ceredigion: www.caehirgardens.com
Chatsworth, Derbyshire: www.chatsworth.org
Coombe Trenchard, Devon: www.coombetrenchard.co.uk
Hestercombe Gardens and Watermill, Somerset: www.hestercombe.com
Stowe Landscape Gardens, Buckinghamshire: www.nationaltrust.org.uk
Ventnor Botanic Gardens, Isle of Wight: www.botanic.co.uk
See also www.britainsfinest.co.uk for more details of dog-friendly gardens to visit.

Index

Dog-friendly gardening

Visit Hubble and Hattie on the web: www.hubblrandhattie.com and www.hubbleandhattie • blogspot.com

f twitter • *Details of all books* • *Special offers* • *Newsletter* • *New book news* •